FROM ANOTHER PLACE

Migration and the politics of culture

GILLIAN BOTTOMLEY

*Associate Professor in Anthropology and Comparative Sociology,
Macquarie University, Sydney*

CAMBRIDGE
UNIVERSITY PRESS

Published by the Press Syndicate of the University of Cambridge
The Pitt Building, Trumpington Street, Cambridge CB2 1RP, UK
40 West 20th Street, New York, NY 10011-4211, USA
10 Stamford Road, Oakleigh, Victoria 3166, Australia

© Cambridge University Press 1992
First published 1992

Printed in Hong Kong by Colorcraft

National Library of Australia cataloguing in publication data
Bottomley, Gillian 1939-   .
From another place : migration and the politics of culture.
Includes index.
ISBN 0 521 41014 2.
1. Emigration and immigration – Social aspects. 2. Culture.
3. Ethnicity. 4. Immigrants – Social conditions. I. Title.
304.82

Library of Congress cataloguing in publication data
Bottomley, Gillian 1939-   .
From another place :
migration and the politics of culture/by Gillian Bottomley.
Includes index.
ISBN 0 521 41014 2.
1. Emigration and immigration – Social aspects. 2. Ethnicity.
3. Australia – Emigration and immigration – Social aspects.
4. Greece – Emigration and immigration – Social aspects. I. Title.
JV6225.B68   1992
304.8 – dc20 91–45061 CIP

A catalogue record for this book is available from the British Library
ISBN 0 521 41014 2 hardback

Contents

Preface and acknowledgements

From Another Place has developed from over twenty years of research and teaching on the subjects of migration, culture, ethnicity and racism, especially on ways of understanding these and their relation to phenomena such as class, gender and relations of power. Most of this research and teaching has taken place in Australia, where over 20 per cent of the inhabitants were born in another country and 25 per cent are of non-Anglophone origin, in a population of over a hundred ethnic groups. The contrast between the diversity of the Australian population and the prevailing Anglocentrism of discourses and practices of knowledge raises intriguing questions about knowledge and power, as well as forms of resistance, adaptation and transformation that can enable people to weave through and across – perhaps even above – these structured power relations.

This Australia-based work has been complemented by extensive comparative research on international migration (see chapters 2 and 3) and related studies in a major country of emigration, Greece (esp. chapters 5, 6 and 7). The framework developed here includes an argument for an international perspective on migration and a comparative understanding of such notions as tradition and ethnicity. The chapters that concentrate on Greece and Greek-Australians within this comparative framework allow for some illumination of both ends of the migration story as well as of the social, economic and cultural networks of the diaspora. At the same time, such a focus has enabled me to explore the rich resources of Greek artistic work – including dance, music and literature – and of ethnographies of Greece, particularly those concerned with gender and the poetics of ethnicity. One of my broader aims here is to interrelate subjective and objective accounts of migration with the experience of difference. Another is to blur the boundaries between various specialist studies, separately defined according to ethnicity, class, migration, gender, culture and so on. I strongly believe that it is the relations (and absences) between and within these forms of studies that should be studied.

Since this project clearly breaches the objective–subjective dimensions of my own life, I have an enormous list of people to whom I am indebted for advice, assistance, encouragement, hospitality, wisdom and support. These include my daughter Fiona, who has shared most of my fieldwork and the consequences of my commitments over the last twenty years; my partner John Lechte, whose integrity and intellectual strength have been sources of inspiration; friends and colleagues, including the late Chandra Jayawardena, Madge Dawson, Marie de Lepervanche, Jeannie Martin, Laki Jayasuriya, Dorothy Buckland, Bob Connell and Vasilis Georgiou in Australia; Nira Yuval-Davis, Floya Anthias and Robert Miles in Britain; Alkis Raftis, Anna Amera, Theo and Patra Patrikareas in Greece, and Michael Herzfeld in the U.S.A. I am also grateful for the enthusiasm and criticisms of my students at Macquarie University, especially those in the courses on migration, race and ethnicity and on the anthropology of the Mediterranean, where a good deal of the material in *From Another Place* was tested and reworked. Macquarie University Research Grants have funded most of my research, supplemented by a grant from the Australian Research Committee for some of the study of second-generation Greek-Australians.

Specific acknowledgements are due to the following people for permission to use material already published. These are: George Papaellinas for the use of parts of his stories, 'The Merchant's Widow', 'Into a Further Dimension' and 'Around the Crate', from his book *Ikons* (1986, Ringwood, Victoria: Penguin Books); Nikos Papastergiadis for part of his poem 'The New Language', published in *Meanjin* in 1986; Π.O. for part of his poem 'Ta!', from pp. 12 and 13 of his *The Fitzroy Poems* (1989, Melbourne: Collective Effort Press). (Extracts from the work of these three authors appear in chapters 4 and 8 below.)

I am also grateful to the following people for permission to use parts of my own previously-published works. Thanks are due to –

Dr Alfred Vincent of the Department of Modern Greek, University of Sydney, for those sections of chapter 5 which appeared in the journal *To Yiofiri* in 1988;

Dr Colette Piault of the Centre Nationale des Recherches Sociales, Paris, for allowing the publication, in revised form in chapter 6, of part of a paper originally included in a book which she directed and edited as *Familles et Biens en Grèce et à Chypre* (1985, Paris: l'Harmattan);

Dr Charles Price of Canberra, for permission to use, in chapter 9, several pages of my contribution to a book which he edited under the title of *Australian National Identity* (1991, Canberra: Academy of the Social Sciences).

GILL BOTTOMLEY

PART I

Migration studies and the problem of culture

CHAPTER 1

Migrations and cultural analyses: a point of departure

... this is, after all, the century of the migrant as well as the century of the bomb, perhaps there have never been so many people who end up elsewhere than they began, whether by choice or by necessity, and so perhaps that's the source from which this kind of reconstruction can begin.

Salman Rushdie, 1987, p.63

Culture is one of the most commonly used concepts in studies of migration, yet it is curiously unexplored. The notion of culture as a way of life of a particular group of people is obviously central to the process of migration, whereby people leave one set of social and historical circumstances and move, or are moved, to another. By this very movement, migration challenges the idea of a distinct way of life. If it is possible to transport whole 'cultures', then their specific conditions of development must be irrelevant. Clearly, this is not the case; anthropological work has long demonstrated the intricate inter-penetrations of economic, political, geographic and social conditions in cultural practices. The process of migration, therefore, calls into question such interrelations between circumstances and practices.

Much of the material about migration and its social consequences demonstrates the considerable difficulty of attempting to answer this question. For example, social scientists often assume that culture = ethnicity, that is, a defined national or linguistic category. Hence we read discussions about multiculturalism or cultural pluralism that concentrate only on 'ethnics', minorities within a state. 'Cultural studies' on the other hand, are more likely to concentrate on class or youth 'subcultures' or on the practices and products of specific classes or class fractions. When these two perspectives are combined, they can provide valuable insights into the construction and transformation of ways of life. Some examples of such successful cross-referencing are Jayawardena's studies of Indian emigration (1963, 1968), Berger's *A Seventh Man* (1975), Piore's *Birds of Passage* (1980), and Gilroy's *There Ain't No Black in the Union Jack* (1987). The theoretical frameworks of these studies differ, but they share certain important similarities. One of these is their concern to interrelate the constraints arising from structured circumstances, caused by migration or by class-based inequalities, with the active construction of cultural practices and the reinterpretation and understanding of both circumstances and practices. Another is their recognition that understanding requires a knowledge of the origins, modes of migration and current circumstances of the subjects of study. In my own studies of Greek-Australians, for example, I have found that international migration can create international people, who identify with kin, friends and fellow emigrants virtually across the world (Bottomley, 1979, 1984). Sociological studies of ethnic minorities often miss the significance of the continuing interaction between homelands and countries of emigration. This neglect can also lead to a reified view of culture, as a kind of package of attributes carried across from the homeland.

I will discuss some of these studies at greater length in the following chapters, which take a basically anthropological approach to culture. Studies of relatively static populations, as many anthropological works have been, are brought into question by migration. But the frameworks used to study migration – derived from demography, political economy, political science, or the sociology of minorities – generally fail to cope adequately with the complexities of culture. The separation of academic disciplines has contributed to this situation, where sociologists see themselves as concerned with the structures of industrial societies, anthropologists with non-industrial societies, political economists with the economic and political bases of social action, and ethnicists with the recovery and development of relatively unproblematic 'traditions'.

The writers I mentioned above all offer inter-disciplinary frameworks, including anthropology, sociology, political economy and, for Berger and Gilroy, a form of poetics. A further similarity is that all these writers include analyses of social power, of the ways in which cultural forms are constructed, dismantled and re-negotiated in the struggle for access to valued resources, for economic and symbolic capital. I will attempt to develop such a perspective on culture in the following chapters. I also believe that it is important to include, with an analysis of structural constraints, the perceptions people have of those constraints. My basic framework here could be described as comparative sociology, derived from anthropology, but seeing the specific instance as 'a particular case of the possible' (cf. Bourdieu, 1986). Anthropologists have developed sophisticated sets of understanding of cultural processes (see Geertz, 1973, Clifford and Marcus, 1986, Herzfeld, 1987). The anthropological method has been described as 'diverse ways of thinking and writing about culture from a standpoint of participant observation' (Clifford, 1988, p.9). Even when this method was at its most objectifying, in the service of colonial governments, it nevertheless required the observer to spend a good deal of time with the observed – the rather sacrosanct activity of fieldwork. Migration studies, on the other hand, are mostly written about the writer's own society and its impact on people within that society who come from other places. But the differences between these two modes of study become increasingly blurred. For example, probably no existing society has been unaffected by industrial civilisation in some way; hence the exotic Other is increasingly a problematic construct. And the decades of intense and continuing international migration have radically altered those immigrant-receiving societies within which studies have been made.

This book includes material gathered from participant observation, as well as from other sources (historical, demographic, statistical, literary, and the work of other social scientists). My participant observation began formally some 22 years ago, with a socio-cultural study of Greek-Australians in Sydney. It has continued through work on southern European settlement in Australia, return migration to Greece, cultural aspects of feminism and political change in Greece and Australia, and, more broadly, through studies of international migration and cultural interactions in industrial societies (Bottomley, 1979, 1983, 1984a, b, c, 1988, 1990).

More informally, I believe that the experience of living in a highly diverse society can generate an intense interest in the processes of cultural formation. For example, during my childhood in a small country town in Australia, the differences and comparisons between the lives of my own family of orientation and the lives of our Aboriginal schoolmates were striking. Many of the Aboriginal children had been deserted by irresponsible fathers, as we had been. Aboriginal mothers and children often lived in economic circumstances not greatly dissimilar to our own. Yet, as descendants of Celtic and European settlers, we had much readier access to the status of 'decent poor', and therefore access to a self-respect denied to the indigenous people – who were, at that time, not allowed into the municipal swimming pool or into the back rows of the cinema. As fringe dwellers in that country town in the 1950s, the Aboriginal people had limited access to the considerable cultural capital of their own heritage, and were forced to endure the status of people who had been deprived of their land and been systematically categorised as 'naturally inferior'.

At the same time, several large and hardworking families of Kytherian Greeks provided another model of family life – somewhat introverted, but solidary and mutually supportive. All our Greek schoolmates belonged to these café-owning families and all became professionals themselves, as a direct result of strong family support. Later I taught at schools in Sydney where one quarter of my students were of non-English-speaking background – a challenging and harrowing experience, but one quite common to teachers in a city where at least one quarter of the population is of non-Anglophone background.

My informal study of migration and culture included emigration from Australia, considerable 'working travel' in Europe, Britain and North America, and several years of employment in Montreal, struggling to communicate in my second language in the fairly hostile environment of Quebec in the early 1960s, when the politics of culture were pervasive (see Handler, 1989, for a detailed academic account). These personal experiences were not academic, of course, but they have shaped my interest in and approach to questions about the processes of cultural formation.

Perhaps even more basically, the experiences of growing up in a poor, mother-headed and all-female household, and of a kind of migration in to the profoundly middle-class (and masculinist) environment of the academy, have also helped me to understand some of the ways in which class and gender structure lifestyles, and are themselves cultural constructs. I will elaborate on these points in later chapters, where I have tried to stress the significance of class and gender perspectives in understanding culture.

In the chapters that follow, I am particularly concerned with the relation between definitions of social power (e.g. based on economic, gender and ethnic criteria) and cultural practices. These discussions offer examples of such interrelations, including studies of international migration and cultural change; of the poetics of ethnicity; of dance, including some political aspects of dance; of the institution of dowry, considered both as tradition and as adaptation; of the cultural construction of gender relations and their links with models of the 'ethnos' or nation; and of the consequences of some of the differences generated by class, gender, age and ethnicity in Australia.

Many of these chapters refer to people of Greek origin, because they are drawn from my own research in Greece and among Greek-Australians. Apart from the fact that Greek-speakers have been international migrants for centuries, they have also actively maintained and translated cultural practices that help to define 'Greekness', even in the diaspora. In Australia's highly diverse population, Greek-speakers make up one of the largest minorities of non-English-speaking background, now extending through several generations (see Bottomley, 1979). There is also a dynamic process of interaction between diaspora Greeks and Greece itself, providing a built-in comparative framework that allows cultural practices to be seen as something other than memories or museum pieces. The very diversity of Australia's population (of over 100 different linguistic groups) raises compelling questions about the politics of culture. I have chosen to concentrate on Greek-speakers because I want to investigate these questions, and concepts such as tradition and ethnicity, through analyses of specific practices. Despite this ethno-specific focus, this is not a comprehensive study of Greek-Australians, nor even of Australian immigration and settlement. The Greek and Australian contexts are rich and interesting in themselves, but my primary intention here is to raise more general questions about migration and settlement and about the constitution and recreation of cultural capital. These studies demonstrate particular cases of a range of possibilities.

In talking about cultural forms, there is a risk of solidifying what should be seen as *process*. 'Culture' is often conceived as products – as books, pieces of music, plays, rituals. My intention here is to emphasise the fluidity of cultural forms, to question static concepts of 'traditions' and 'institutions', and to try to reveal something of the flow of social relations in cultural processes.

The chapters that follow range across a number of social fields, from considerations of dance and music to studies of gender relations and representations of race and ethnicity. A common thread running throughout is an exploration of what might be called muted modes.

This is a similar usage to that of 'muted models', referred to by Ardener (1975) and Dubisch (1986). Muted models have been described as 'muted in the face of the dominant ideology' and perhaps 'only vaguely articulated by the members of the subordinate group themselves' (Dubisch, 1986, p.32). But the term 'model' implies a conscious construct, whereas certain modes of expression and communication may be barely conscious, perhaps literally embodied, as in dance, or hardly surfacing in a discourse (as, I would argue, the poetics of ethnicity rarely appear in social scientific studies of migration). One of my aims is to develop different ways of perceiving and perhaps understanding such modes, of listening to voices that tend to be subdued and raising questions about absences.

I am aware of the dangers in such a project, of the criticisms of writers such as Edward Said of those who apparently claim to represent others (see Said, 1978, 1985). These are criticisms with which I am familiar, as an Anglophone who has written extensively about migration to Australia. The area of migration studies is inherently political, and it is difficult to avoid the pitfalls of insider–outsider debates. Said has also pointed to a 'kind of possessive exclusivism . . . the sense of being an excluding insider by virtue of experience . . . or by virtue of method', i.e. only women or migrants can write about women and migrants, only Marxists or feminists can write about economics or women's literature, and so on (ibid., p.15). My position here is that both domination and understanding can take many forms, and that both experience and methods are therefore comparable. But both should be scrutinised critically, rather than assuming understanding either through some kind of essentialism or through methodological orthodoxy. Perhaps the ultimate test of intellectual work here is the response from those whom we appear to represent. I have certainly found it a challenging, stimulating and instructive experience to have my work constantly discussed, criticised and evaluated by the 'subjects' of my research, over the last fifteen years or so.

In fact, one of the continuing themes in these chapters is a resistance to ready categorising, a resistance that becomes apparent in the ways in which people perceive and act on structural forms and limitations. Such resistances may create their own contradictions, as Paul Willis demonstrated in his study of 12 working class 'lads' who, in rejecting schooling as an avenue to social mobility, virtually ensured that they were thoroughly adapted to factory work (Willis, 1981). In my own research, I have argued that the resources of

'Greekness' have offered Greek-Australians a positive sense of identity in the face of the negative pressures towards assimilation (cf. Bottomley, 1979, 1987). However, these forms of Greekness can include their own processes of subjection that also generate resistance. For example, family relations may reflect mutually contradictory pressures – the family is central to Greekness, especially in Australia, yet the State, the economy and more general ideas about personal freedom are based on individualism (cf. Strintzos, 1984; Bottomley, 1984a). And the tolerance of 'difference' promoted in policies of multiculturalism blends into notions of individual differences that can generate conflict within the 'imagined communities' that construct and guard ethnic identities. The difficulty, then, lies in developing a framework that can help us to understand some of these complexities, rather than to resort too easily to formulae about one or other perspective or category – such as either class, ethnicity, or gender.

In the light of these remarks, the title of the book may be a little clearer. I am arguing from some slightly different perspectives on the subjects discussed here. These chapters are critical in the sense that they all question legitimated ways of understanding and representing the social world. They also suggest other ways of understanding, partly by attempting to hear muted modes, and partly by presenting material from another perspective.

Much of this material is about others of several kinds, especially that part drawn from Greece or Greek-Australians. But my main focus of study is the work of other academics and scholars. My central critiques are of representations of culture, of the static notion of tradition, of the narrowing effect of dichotomous schemata used to describe social relations, of views on migration and ethnicity, and, finally, paraphrasing John Berger, 'ways of knowing'.

The material is heterogeneous, but it refracts the themes of culture and social power from several different viewpoints – in general, from the perspectives of those who, in one or more senses, come from another place, those who are not the 'natural' legitimators of social knowledge. The perspectives offered here may also be misrepresentations but the main aim of my project is to question certainties rather than offer an alternative Truth.

As a university teacher, I am myself part of a powerful legitimating structure, of course. However, my perception of universities is not that of one who feels at home. As Bourdieu's brilliant study of class-based universes demonstrates, a 'sense of one's place' appears as natural in those whose conditions of existence have produced particular practices and lifestyles (1986). Bourdieu's notion of 'habitus', 'history turned into nature' (1977, p.78), which generates practices and perceptions, will be an important organising concept in several chapters, and I will discuss it further in the next few pages.

In my own case, habitus helps to explain a tangential and sometimes resistant perspective, developed as a rural 'poor white' female and, more academically, as an evening student at a university that barely tolerated such a marginal species. I mention these conditions in order to point out that I am also, in some ways, from another place. My particular life experiences are surprisingly remote to most academics, even to many who have an abstract understanding of the existence of poverty, of gender- and regionally-based inequalities and the elitism of universities. Despite claims to egalitarianism, there are real, lasting and basic cultural differences generated by our relations to class-based conditions. In a way, the limits of necessity create, in James Baldwin's phrase, 'another country'.

At the same time, differences generated in this way can be valuable in relativising claims to legitimacy: the absence of shared assumptions can bring such assumptions into question. I have heard the same observation from a number of people who have experienced the much more profound alienation of migration, but also from others whose class habitus means that a university is not naturally 'their' place. 'Different definitions of the impossible, the possible, and the probable, cause one group to experience as natural or reasonable practices or aspirations which another group finds unthinkable or scandalous, and vice versa' (Bourdieu, 1977, p.78).

Nevertheless, I make no claim to special insider knowledge of a particular category of people, not even on the basis of sisterhood, as some might argue (cf. Strathern, 1985). I share some objectives and some understanding with some of the people in this book but, above all, my own experience and that of my family underlie an interest in the operation of power relations and, especially, in forms of resistance and creative modifications.

THE POLITICS OF CULTURE

The chapters of this book all pose questions about the politics of culture. My working definition of culture is borrowed from Raymond Williams: 'a constitutive social process creating specific and different ways of life' (1977, p.19). I would add to this definition Stuart Hall's note that culture includes

both the meanings and values which arise amongst distinctive social groups and classes, on the basis of their given historical conditions and relationships, through which they handle and respond to the conditions of existence; *and* the lived traditions and practices through which those 'understandings' are expressed and in which they are embodied. (1981, p.26)

In *Keywords* (1976) and *Culture* (1981), Williams describes the concept of culture as one of the most difficult in the language. Certainly, it is used with considerable variation. It is, however, worth following his brief history of the concept from its early use as a noun of process – as we still find it in 'horticulture' and 'agriculture' – to a noun of configuration or generalisation, a kind of informing spirit of a whole way of life, manifest in all social activities but especially in language, styles of art, and intellectual work. It was taken up in this sense by anthropologists, and provides a valuable sense of the interconnectedness of social activities. However, the concept tended to support a rather static view of cultures as integrated and enduring wholes that could 'clash' on contact or be completely destroyed. There are several problems with this view. One is that human history has been one of constant cultural interaction, interchange and change. This means that cultural processes are always historically specific. To quote Eric Wolf:

We need to remember that the culture concept came to the fore in a specific historical context, during a period when some European nations were contending for dominance while others were striving for separate identities and independence. The demonstration that each struggling nation possessed a distinctive society, animated by its special spirit or culture, served to legitimate its aspirations to form a separate state of its own. The notion of separate and integral cultures responded to this political project. Once we locate the reality of society in historically changing, imperfectly bounded, multiple and branching social alignments, however, the concept of a boxed, unitary and bounded culture must give way to a sense of the fluidity and permeability of cultural sets. In the rough and tumble of social interaction, groups are known to exploit the ambiguities of inherited forms, to impart new evaluations or valences to them, to borrow forms more expressive of their interests, or to create wholly new forms in answer to changed circumstances. Furthermore, if we think of such interaction not as causative in its own terms but as responsive to larger economic and political forces, the explanation of cultural forms must take account of that larger context, that wider field of force. A 'culture' is thus better seen as a series of processes that construct, reconstruct and dismantle cultural materials, in response to identifiable determinants. (1982, p.387)

As I argued earlier, concepts such as culture and society objectify processes that are partly the outcome of people's perceptions and appreciation of their worlds. What Bourdieu describes as the 'structuralist moment' is necessary because the truth of social interaction is never entirely in the interaction as observed, and we must recognise the structural constraints on perceptions. But actions and interactions cannot be deduced from structures (1987).

Williams, like Bourdieu, criticises the excessive objectivism that separates so-called society from culture. In his words,

Society is never only the dead husk which limits social and individual fulfilment. It is also always a constitutive process with very powerful pressures which are both expressed in political, economic and cultural formations and internalised to become individual wills. (1977, p.88)

According to Williams, the Marxist separation of base and super-structure prevents us from understanding the production and reproduction of social and political forms. It also implies a kind of homogeneity of conditions, and tends to assume a unity of groups, where there are in fact conflicts, divisions and alternative definitions of reality. Cultural practices are related to specific distributions of power and influence by the hegemonic process that effectively 'saturates' the whole process of living to such a degree that the pressures and limits of a specific economic, political and cultural system 'seem to most of us the pressures and limits of simple experience and common sense' (1977, p.11). But this hegemonic process is also resisted, modified and altered by other pressures. 'The reality of cultural process must then always include the efforts and contributions of those who are in one way or another outside or at the edge of the terms of the specific hegemony' (1977, p.113).

The cultural process is, therefore, inherently political. Not only do people reconstruct, dismantle and resist what Wolf calls 'cultural sets of practices and ideas' (1982, p.391), but they do so in the context of competition for economic and symbolic capital. The most elaborated study of this competition is Bourdieu's *Distinction: A Social Critique of the Judgement of Taste* (1986). In his detailed and multiplex analysis, Bourdieu reveals the ways in which tastes function as markers of class. Art and cultural consumption are, he argues, predisposed to legitimate social differences. Bourdieu has always paid particular attention to the play of power relations in the social field, to the ways in which things are done and perceived as well as their apparent objectivity. What appear as differences in life style are, according to his analysis, positions in the field of power. In fact, those who occupy similar positions have every chance of possessing similar dispositions and interests, a similar 'sense of one's place'. This sense of place is literally embodied, i.e. written on the body, in language and in particular ways of being-in-the-world. Those who dominate, therefore, appear as distinguished because of their distinguished positions. Their socially-constituted natures are immediately adjusted to the game, 'naturally'. They are not identifiable by distinguished conduct, as Veblen suggested, but by the 'ontological complicity' of what Bourdieu calls *habitus* (1987, p.40).

The concept of habitus helps to break down the subject/object dichotomy. It is 'history become nature', an intermediary between social positions and practices that represent the world as structured. Habitus is an objective relation between practices and situation that produces meaning through categories of perception and appreciation that are themselves socially produced.

Thus . . . the habitus acquired in the family underlies the structuring of the school experience . . . and the habitus transformed by schooling, itself diversified, in turn underlies the structuring of our subsequent experiences . . . and so on, from restructuring to restructuring. (1977, pp.86–7)

So objective relations of power tend to reproduce themselves in relations of symbolic power. The struggle to monopolise the legitimate symbolic system raises issues of representation. Bourdieu argues that the power to 'make groups' is political power *par excellence*. What Benedict Anderson describes as 'imagined communities' (1983) exist if people exist who can represent such a community and be recognised by those who see themselves as represented (cf. Bourdieu, 1987).

Bourdieu also directs attention to the ways in which social categories and classifications organise our perceptions of the world, especially as they operate through dichotomous oppositions such as male–female; high–low; light–darkness. The self-evident nature of such symbolic systems disguises their political dimension.

In the chapters that follow, I will address some of these issues. First, I compare some of the sociological work on migration, ethnicity and 'race' in the United States and Britain, in order to locate *From Another Place* in relation to these studies. The main themes to be traced throughout this book – an international perspective, an anthropological approach, the inclusion of subjective as well as objective accounts, a recognition of class and gender – will be discussed in relation to the U.S. and U.K. material. Chapter 3 examines the concept of culture in studies of migration and ethnicity. I am concerned here with the ways in which 'culture' has been used, but also with the operation of the politics of culture, in the terms already described – as part of the struggle for symbolic power and part of the constitution of specific ways of life.

Chapters 4, 5 and 6 analyse some of these specific ways of life. The discussions of dance and music and of dowry reveal some aspects of the operation of social power in practices that tend to be regarded as apolitical. They also capture something of the dismantling and re-assembling of cultural forms, referred to by Eric Wolf. In these chapters, I scrutinise some interpretations of these practices, and the resort to concepts like 'folk' and 'tradition' as a way of categorising, abstracting and even subjecting the practices thus described.

The available paradigms for understanding the cultural construction of gender relations in Greece and some of the contradictions and resistances that emerge from anthropological and sociological studies are examined in chapter 7. One of the central themes of this chapter is that of 'Greek identity' and the constitution of the ethnos. As I argued earlier, this sort of theme is important in migration studies, but is usually explored only in the context of the country of immigration. My aim here is to indicate some of the intersections of gender relations and cultural practices in Greece as a guide to a deeper understanding of related practices in the diaspora. Chapters 8 and 9 offer a view of Australian society from an unusual perspective, of those who, in Williams' words, are somewhat at the edge of the hegemonic processes of that society. Accordingly, these chapters analyse some of the ways in which, for example, the second generation, elderly people, women and migrants are represented by social scientists, health workers and policy makers. This is not merely a negative critique, however. As in other chapters, an important contribution is the construction of alternative models of understanding.

These last three chapters also develop some general questions about gender and power relations. Culturally-constructed gender relations operate as one of the major axes of social power in most, if not all societies. Men have more formal power than women and, in many cases, the forms of this power are among the most significant diacritical features of a specific cultural formation. For example, the seclusion of women, their submissiveness, the embodiment of power relations in their dress and bearing, can signify the cultural distinctiveness of a society, as they do in the Ayatollahs' Iran at present. Under conditions of less extreme political fervour, gender is intricately connected to other forms of social relations. In these final chapters, I draw out some of those interconnections.

Parts of these may be familiar to some readers, having appeared, in different forms, as sections of conference papers, lectures, journal articles or book chapters over the last eight or nine years, during the course of my research and teaching on the politics of culture. Some overlap is unavoidable, but all chapters have been reformulated and integrated within the framework of this book, in order to allow discussion and interrelation of a fairly diverse range of material.

For me, the politics of culture have been most successfully analysed by such writers as Athol Fugard, Nadine Gordimer, Salman Rushdie, Italo Calvino and Patrick White. Sociological analyses are bound to be more limited and less enthralling than these, yet they can also reveal some of the limits of necessity and offer an enhanced understanding of the way people experience, define and respond to their conditions of life. I believe that literature is necessary to sociology in several ways. Perhaps the most important of these is in literature's capacity for self-criticism. As Calvino has pointed out,

We can no longer neglect the fact that books are made of words, of signs, of methods of construction – that books often say something different from what they set out to say, that in any book there is a part that is the author's and a part that is a collective and anonymous work. (1982, p.99)

Calvino compares literature to politics, but we can extend the reference to include the broadly defined sociology discussed here. To paraphrase Calvino, much of sociology is also verbal construction, myth and literary *topos*. Like literature, sociology must 'above all know itself and distrust itself' (1982, p.100).

CHAPTER 2

Comparative studies of migration, ethnicity, 'race' and culture in the United States and Britain

> The history which bears and determines us has the form of a
> war rather than that of language: relations of power, not
> relations of meaning. History has no 'meaning', though this
> is not to say that it is absurd or incoherent. On the contrary, it
> is intelligible and should be susceptible to analysis down to
> the smallest detail, but this in accordance with the
> intelligibility of struggles, of strategies and tactics.
>
> Foucault, quoted in Lipsitz, 1990, p.30

Many of the examples and contextual studies used in this book come from Greece or Australia. As we will see, migration has been central to the histories and cultural formation of both countries. Chapters 1 and 3 sketch a comparative framework for these specific analyses, but I also want to relate them more closely to some of the migration studies undertaken in other milieux, partly in order to argue for the general heuristic value of the approach that I will develop. I described this approach as 'comparative sociology', but it can have implications for political economists, political scientists and educationists as well as for scholars and practitioners concerned with settlement programs and cultural production and with individual lives. The integration of structural, cultural and subjective dimensions throughout these chapters will require the crossing of disciplinary boundaries.

In fact, the study of migration raises issues central to the development of the social sciences: understanding modernity, the rise of industrialism, rural–urban population movements, the creation of urban working classes from peasantries – all demonstrated in the work of founding fathers such as Marx, Durkheim, Weber, Toennies, and Simmel. It is also central to more contemporary questions about post-modernity, post-industrialism, the fragmentation of working classes, the consequences of uneven development and the interrelation of political, social and cultural systems. Yet a great deal of the study of migration has been marginalised and compartmentalised in the social sciences into specialties such as ethnic, racial or minority studies. In this process, wider issues have been lost or submerged, along with the interconnections between these artificial specialisms. Too often, the social questions of the early European theorists have been dissolved into the questionnaires of empiricist academic social scientists. I am arguing here for a return to the larger questions, about the cultural composition of industrial societies with hetero-geneous populations, the interaction between those populations and their various countries and cultures of origin, the flow of power relations between definitions of social power (e.g. based on economic, gender and ethnic criteria) and cultural practices, and the formation of personal and group identities. These questions cast doubt on analyses based on uni-dimensional explanations such as *either* class *or* ethnicity, on a focus only on countries of immigration, and on static concepts of culture as tradition. In discussing the relevance to other studies of the approach used in this book, I will cover the following themes:

(a) an international perspective, interrelating countries of emigration and immigration, and their populations;
(b) the origins of migrants and their location within economic, political and social structures of countries of immigration;
(c) the place of anthropological studies in understanding both (a) and (b) above;
(d) the inclusion of the subjective in studies of migration and settlement, especially in literary and other artistic forms of expression.

These, mostly substantive, themes will intersect with more theoretical considerations, such as:

(a) an understanding of culture as social processes which can be analysed in the construction of class and gender, as well as ethnic relations;
(b) the interrelations of objective and subjective accounts;
(c) some recognition of migrants as agents, who act upon, adapt and resist structured circumstances;
(d) the development of a gender perspective.

Bearing these eight themes in mind, I will briefly discuss some of the research undertaken in the U.S.A. and U.K., in order to locate my own approach in relation to some of those developed in these important centres of immigration and migration studies. My intention here is to take a long view of the work of social scientists, rather than to participate in current debates, or to summarise the 'current state of play'.

MIGRATION AND THE U.S.A.

Immigration is a kind of charter myth in contemporary U.S.A. culture, as basic to the formation of the American nation. At the level of artistic expression, it is immediately apparent that some of the greatest American writers, artists and musicians have been immigrants or had immigrant parents. Much of their work has been explicitly concerned with immigration and the experience of minorities. Saul Bellow's writings, for example, always include characters who negotiate multiple sign systems and whose friendships, kin networks and memories stretch across the world or deep into ghetto life. Bellow can condense multiple facets of the lived experience of class and migration into a few elegant sentences. In *Mr Sammler's Planet,* talking about Elya Gruner, who migrated from Poland as a child, he conveys some of the shadings of class and ethnicity that have coloured Gruner's life.

Dr Gruner himself had grown up in a hoodlum neighbourhood and sometimes dropped into the hoodlum manner, speaking out of the corner of his mouth. He was a widower. His wife had been a German Jewess, above him socially, so she thought. Her family had been 1848 pioneers. Gruner was an Ostjude immigrant. Her job was to refine him, to help him build his practice. The late Mrs. Gruner had been decent, proper, with thin legs, bouffant hair sprayed stiffly, and Peck & Peck outfits, geometrically correct to the millimetre. Gruner had believed in the social superiority of his wife. (Bellow, 1971, pp.63–4)

Among many more examples of such insightful works are those of Vladimir Nabokov, whose superb *Pnin* (1960) embodies the experience of foreignness with tremendous dignity and compassion. Maxine Hong Kingston's books, *China men* (1980) and *The Woman Warrior* (1976), explore the re-creation of the immigrants' past, and the stories and customs used by the parental generation to define Chinese-American experience. Her examination of these 'stories' allows for an interweaving and questioning of the Chinese and American parts of her own life and the wider implications of the status of Chinese-Americans.

As I suggested in chapter 1 (and will demonstrate in later chapters), creative work of this kind can offer insights not available in social science studies. It can reveal valuable internal perspectives on the kind of reconstruction that follows migration, as well as giving a voice to people who may, because of language, foreignness or relative powerlessness, be without a voice. It also demonstrates the resistances and agency of people who are, in more external accounts, often seen as hapless victims of circumstance. And it throws light on the receiving societies, from the valleys rather than the commanding heights of those societies – the positions (more or less) occupied by social scientists.

Some historians have tackled the question of the broader cultural and political consequences of being a nation of immigrants. According to Kolko (1976) and Karabel (1979), migration is central to U.S.A. history and immigrant workers formed the heart of the American working class in the crucial formative years from 1870 to 1930. The results of this mass immigration were high pressure working conditions, deskilling of labour, ethnic fragmentation of the workforce and the development of an ethnic rather than a class consciousness. The decentralised political system emphasised locality and patronage networks. Karabel (1979) and, later, Howe (1986) see these tendencies as partly accounting for the failure of socialism in the U.S.A., where, according to Howe, they were reinforced by the national myth of America as humanity's second chance, a 'New Israel'. These accounts of U.S.A. political and economic history are much more informative and dynamic than Hartz's rather essentialist but influential notions about fragments of the old country defining the political cultures of settler societies (cf. Hartz, 1964). Gutman's study (1976) of work, culture and society in industrialising America is even richer in its examination of the *processes* by which 'pre-modern' workers were incorporated into the development of industrialism. Gutman, following the anthropologist, Sidney Mintz, sees culture as a kind of 'resource', and society as a 'kind of arena', concepts not unlike Bourdieu's notion of symbolic and cultural capital and social field, which I use in several of the chapters of this book. Within this framework, Gutman examines the transformation of pre-industrial work habits (for example, celebrations, and a different notion of time) into the habits required of industrial workers. Their resistance often took a violent form, including attacks on machinery and property, food riots and bitter strikes reminiscent of agrarian uprisings. Police and domestic military were increasingly organised for the purpose of creating and controlling industrial workers, and there have been constant moves to legislate or 'guide' morality. Gutman quotes a handbook for immigrant Jews in the 1890s, advising them to . . . 'hold fast . . . forget your past, your customs and your ideals . . . do not take a moment's rest. Run, do, work, and keep your own good in mind' (1976, p.69).

Those historians who argued for the centrality of migration were not, however, the most influential writers on the subject of U.S.A. history. Karabel (1979) explicitly criticised the prevailing 'frontier thesis', which explained history in terms of geographic mobility and the expansiveness of a frontier ethic, rather than the kind of political and economic conflict integral to the model used by Kolko, Karabel and Gutman. That conflict model, however, resembles those used by the sociologists Sennett and Cobb (in *Hidden Injuries of Class*, 1972) and Steinberg (*The Ethnic Myth*, 1981). I shall return to these two important studies after a brief historical excursion into the sociological study of U.S.A. immigration.

Sociology in the U.S.A. developed from the American Social Science Association, founded in the mid-nineteenth century by social reformists, who, in Birnbaum's words, were 'horrified by the immigrant slums and determined to ascertain the dimensions of the mess before cleaning it up' (1971, p.206). Highly influential in this process was the work of Chicago sociologists, Park and Burgess, whose *Introduction to the Science of Sociology* (1921) discussed the concepts of status and role that were later developed in Parsons' highly elaborated systems theory. Although Park and Burgess were also concerned with competition between groups and individuals, Park postulated a somewhat mechanistic 'cyclical theory of race relations', whereby groups passed through phases of competition, conflict, co-operation and accommodation (see Newman, 1973). This theory fitted the prevailing policies of assimilation, or 'melting pot', although some of the detailed studies made by these scholars actually revealed pervasive conflicts. For example, Thomas and Znaniecki's *Polish Peasant in Europe and America* (1918) and Wirth's *The Ghetto* (1928) demonstrated both the marginalising of immigrants and the oppressiveness entailed in making peasants into industrial workers. But these themes were not drawn out by the earlier sociologists, as they were by later writers such as Gutman, Kolko and Steinberg.

This differing emphasis was partly a consequence of their respective theoretical frameworks. The early sociologists were concerned with individuals or small groups rather than the structures of American society. But they also saw the immigrants' problems as temporary, or as evidence of a cultural pluralism that did not necessarily imply in-built inequalities. This kind of culturalism has been pervasive, encouraging the study of migration and settlement as a measurement of attitudes and values, ignoring the constraints of political and economic systems that pre-exist and pre-define immigrants' status. Park and Burgess, for example, defined assimilation as

... a process of interpenetration and fusion in which persons and groups acquire the memories, sentiments and attitudes of other persons or groups and, by sharing their experience and history, are incorporated with them in a common cultural life. (1921, p.735)

These memories, sentiments and attitudes are obviously seen as freely shared. They are not defined by opposition, hierarchy or exclusion, not used as markers of distinction or of symbolic power. In practice, as we have seen, assimilation policies inevitably include attempts to destroy and devalue the memories and attitudes of immigrants.

Surprisingly little comparative work was undertaken by these earlier sociologists, either by comparing countries of origin with the U.S.A. or by comparing ethnic groups. Lloyd Warner and Leo Srole were later writers who produced a comprehensive study, *The Social Systems of American Ethnic Groups* (1945). This study showed the basic importance of economic security, 'the only security attainable to a stranger in a new social world' (p.7), with capital and goods providing the avenue to status and power. Warner and Srole also considered the motivation to migrate as one of the factors retarding or accelerating status mobility. Other factors were family structure, order of appearance in the U.S.A., proximity to homeland, size of ethnic population, and similarities between the immigrants and the host population.

Despite its emphasis on consensus, this is an interesting study, with detailed analyses of family and organisational structures and a clear understanding of the power of the dominant WASP ethic in U.S.A. society. Warner and Srole were also aware of other systems of domination, such as the patriarchal structures they describe within Greek-American families. Lloyd Warner had earlier written about the barriers to economic advancement thrown up against black Americans, and went so far as to argue that a caste system existed in the U.S.A., with boundaries defined by colour (Warner, 1936). I shall return to this point.

Warner and Srole's study provides a kind of counterpoint to the work of the most influential sociologist of the time, Talcott Parsons, whose intricately constructed and totalising systems theory almost entirely ignored ethnic differences, while reducing them, along with gender and class-based differences, to problems of 'the institutionalisation of role-expectations' and 'the integration of stable systems of social interaction' – in other words, to the problem of the maintenance of social order (see Parsons, 1951). Parsons' later work (for example, in Glazer and Moynihan, 1975) shows a more acute awareness of the differences within American society, but his earlier systems model has had far-reaching effects throughout the world, where, in Birnbaum's words, it has served as 'an ancillary technique of bureaucratic domination' (1971, p.221).

Writing in 1959, C. Wright Mills criticised two tendencies among sociologists in the U.S.A. One, the Parsonian variant, he labelled 'Grand Theory' and the second 'Abstracted Empiricism'. The first of these, Mills argued, never descends from higher generalities to 'problems in their historical and structural contexts' (p.33); Grand Theorists fetishise concepts. The second tendency, Abstracted Empiricism, has an overriding concern with method (usually called 'methodology', perhaps because the Ancient Greek adds distinction). Social theory, in this tendency, consists of concepts useful for analysing statistical findings. But the method and the data often become ends in themselves. The links between wider theory, method and data may not have been made.

One of the reasons for the development of these two tendencies in U.S.A. sociology was a pervasive exclusion of Marxist thought, which could have (and has since) directed attention to the struggle for social power and the interplay of material interests and spiritual values in societies. Parsons' own use of Weber's work was also rather selective, compared, for example to the Weberian references of C. Wright Mills. From the point of view of migration studies, these two tendencies encouraged marginalisation. The consensus view of systems theorists suggested an inevitable incorporation and assimilation of differences, and the separation of empirical from theoretical work led to the subdivision of sociology into specialisms such as 'ethnic studies', where description and a concern with detail can fail to raise questions about the nature of society or the social and political relations within which 'ethnicity' exists.

Several important studies did raise such questions in the early 1960s, two being Gordon's *Assimilation in American Life* (1964) and Glazer and Moynihan's *Beyond the Melting Pot* (1963). Glazer and Moynihan found that ethnic groups were not melting, as planned, but re-forming and transforming their original sources of identity. Gordon also considered social class, and stressed the importance of 'equal civil rights for all, regardless of race, religion or national background . . .' (1964, p.265). Both books, however, demonstrate a consensual view of society and eschew a critique of social inequality.

In 1972, the sociologists Richard Sennett and Jonathan Cobb developed such a critique in their book, *The Hidden Injuries of Class*. Challenging the assumption that material affluence bred political quietism, they sought an explanation of political conservatism in terms of the historic isolation of working class Americans, their immigrant origins, orientation towards the homeland, the displace-ment of native workers and accompanying hostility, which forced immigrants back into ethnic communities and family life. Within a wider study of the consequences of class structure in U.S.A. society, Sennett and Cobb described the migrants' integration into a world with different symbols of respect and courtesy from those that existed in ethnic enclaves. Prevailing ideas about the possibilities of achievement and about meritocracy place the burden of success or failure on individuals themselves, obscuring the structured un-freedom of class positions. The very processes described by Karabel and Gutman – of residential clustering, the development of local and ethnic political identification rather than one based on class, the attachment to the political system through the neighbourhood rather than the workplace – all combined to leave people of immigrant background without grounds for solidarity when urban renewal programs and real estate costs began to break up what Gans (1962) described as 'urban villages'.

Sennett and Cobb's book was important in breaking through the general consensus model in sociology, in locating their detailed interview- and observation-based data within a theoretical framework that took up issues of historical and social change and divisions within American society. In terms of the four substantive themes I outlined at the beginning of this chapter, *The Hidden Injuries of Class* included three – the place of immigrants and their offspring in economic, political and social structures in the U.S.A.; a detailed study of values, beliefs and aspirations of the people they studied compared with those of the host society, and some account of life in the U.S.A. from the point of view of their immigrant subjects. Sennett and Cobb also made good use of more detailed, anthropological studies like Gans' *Urban Villagers* (1962), Berger's *Working Class Suburb* (1968) and Willmott's *Adolescent Boys of East London* (1966).

Some of the themes in *The Hidden Injuries of Class* were taken up by Steinberg in *The Ethnic Myth: race, ethnicity and class in America* (1981), which I will discuss more fully in chapter 4. Steinberg criticised the earlier sociologists' emphasis on measures of acculturation, pointing out that 'cultural differences properly mark the beginning, not the end, of social analysis, and it is necessary to carry the analysis a step further by investigating their historical and social sources' (p.83). He argued that the literature of the ethnic pluralists devotes little space to the problem of inequality, although the pluralist model assumes a basic equality. When ethnicity co-exists with class disadvantage, 'then powerful inducements exist for the members of such groups to assimilate into the mainstream culture, since this will improve their chances for a better life' (p.256). The consequent destruction of ethnic subcultures was not just the outcome of cultural repression, but part of the immigrants' own quests for 'success' and, at times, survival. To Steinberg, however, the ultimate ethnic myth is 'the belief that the cultural symbols of the past can provide more than a comfortable illusion to shield us from present day discontents' (p.262). Like Sennett and Cobb, Steinberg covered several of the themes outlined at the beginning of this chapter, although he, along with most scholars in migration studies, focussed on the receiving society to the neglect of the international implications of these massive migration movements.

An important and eclectic study of U.S.A. migration within an international perspective was Piore's *Birds of Passage* (1979). Piore developed a multifocal approach to the study of migrant labour and industrial societies. This approach allows readers to move between the wide view of international economics and politics and the interrelations between sending and receiving countries and the narrower focus on the lives of immigrants and their offspring. The main shortcomings of this book, from my own point of view, are in the relatively unquestioning approach to culture, but this is a matter of focus and primary interest. Piore did, however, examine some of the material about the 'culture of poverty', which is, at its worst, a cultural determinist explanation of the enduring nature of poverty in the U.S.A.

As an economist, Piore was primarily concerned with economic theories of labour migration. However, he argued cogently for an alternative approach to the study of migrant labour, to consider 'aspects of socio-economic behaviour from which orthodox theory explicitly abstracts and deliberately neglects' (1979, p.7). In keeping with this approach, Piore paid close attention to the experience of migrant workers. In chapter 3, he looked at the dual lives of workers, as *homo economicus* (migrants) and as themselves (at home). The money earned as migrants is often needed for status improvements at home, and this fact has important implications for sending countries. As John Berger did in *A Seventh Man* (1975) (see chapter 3 below), Piore explored the ways in which the image of the receiving country is enhanced and reinforced in countries of emigration (p.58). Piore advocated the use of detailed, more anthropological studies of immigrant populations for deeper understanding of communal relations and integration, as well as of the disruption of migration, where the individual is placed outside a structured social context and is forced to develop such a context. In chapter 5, he returned to cultural explanations in looking at the impact of migration on the immigrants' place of origin, criticising the assumption that emigration has led to economic development in these countries. Reflecting on the movement of returned emigrants into entrepreneurial work, Piore referred to the peasant traditions of independence that helped the 'old' migrants to establish themselves in countries such as the U.S.A., and more recent migrants to re-establish themselves back home. Piore also insisted that accounts of migration to and settlement in receiving countries are incomplete without some analysis of the other half of the picture, the country of emigration.

In such a brief account of the U.S.A. material, I have virtually omitted the subject of 'race'. To some extent, such an omission follows the separation of migration and race studies, a separation rendered problematic by the facts that Afro-Americans were a first wave of forced migrant labour and that the focus of racism is not, of course, confined to black Americans. Migration, ethnicity and racism are closely associated in practice, and have been more closely linked in more recent work, such as that of Steinberg. I have already mentioned Steinberg's (and Gordon's) argument that the rise of interest in ethnicity was related to the rising consciousness and political activity of Afro-Americans. Black Americans are also listed as an ethnic group in the census, and their low status, as the group with the second lowest family income, strongly challenges the high ideals of democratic pluralism. As one black writer expressed it, 'at no moment in my life have I ever felt as though I were American' (Toni Morrison, quoted in Hacker, 1988). Hacker summarises some of the circumstances giving rise to this feeling of being 'an alien in your own land':

The sheer strain of such an existence takes its toll in many ways. The high incidence of drug addiction and crime, of broken families and out-of-wedlock births, of unfinished education and sporadic employment – all seem to me connected with the tensions of living surrounded by a largely hostile culture. Blacks are from six to seven times more likely to end up serving prison terms; they also enter mental institutions at twice the white rate. Their incidence of diabetes, nephritis, and hypertension is double that for whites; and the odds of a black becoming a homicide victim are four times the national figure. However much blacks are held accountable for these conditions, who can doubt that white society is deeply culpable in not addressing them? White Americans have still to ask themselves one decisive question: How would they have fared in their own country had they been born black? (1988, p.41)

This question takes us back to Warner's suggestion that a caste system based on colour exists in the U.S.A. Warner was soundly opposed by Oliver Cromwell Cox, who linked racism to the development of a class society, thus intricately tied to the rise of capitalism and the exploitation of slave labour (see Cox, 1948). But Gunnar Myrdal, in his monumental study of 'The Negro Problem and Modern Democracy' (*An American Dilemma*, first published in 1944), unhesitatingly described a caste system in the social relations between black and white Americans, based particularly on the traditions of slavery. Much more recent work, such as Blauner's longitudinal study, *Black Lives, White Lives* (1989), generally confirms the existence of profound differences in understanding and experience between his interviewees, based on colour more than on class. In fact, Blauner argues that many of the benefits that blacks have fought for over the last three decades have accompanied a recognition of separation, even within classes.

For our purposes here, it is important to note the early linking of concepts such as class, caste and racism, also present in the work of Franklin Frazier in the 1940s and 1950s. It was Frazier who made the point that American sociologists had contributed surprisingly little to the study of race (Frazier, 1947). Clearly, this is no longer true, but Blauner's work, especially, shows the importance of recognising the fact that political struggles include competition for symbolic and cultural capital. Black Americans share very little of the kind of cultural capital represented by education, for example. But in some forms of cultural expression, black Americans have notably surpassed their white compatriots; the outstanding example being jazz, internationally regarded as a major contribution of 'American culture'. Writers like James Baldwin and Alice Walker, dancers like Alvin Ailey and musicians like Billie Holliday also 'speak' with great force about the politics of resistance and subjection (including that form of subjection based on gender – resoundingly absent from most studies of migration, race and ethnicity). More recently, black American music has combined with African and Caribbean music to dominate popular music worldwide (Gilroy, 1988/89).

In *The Afro-centric Idea* (1989), Molefi Kete Asante, a professor of African American Studies, describes the rhetoric and rhythm of black life, seeing the musical concept of beat as a 'path to transcendence', even in the game of basketball. One of the problems with the argument advanced by Asante is that the Eurocentric standpoint, which he criticises, thoroughly dominates evaluation of and rewards for achievement in the U.S.A. Andrew Hacker reinforces this point in his analysis of the struggle for symbolic capital currently under way in the American education system, on behalf of Spanish-speaking and Asian immigrants as well as Afro-Americans. Hacker raises basic questions about employment possibilities, and higher education, but also about the salience of ethnicity in the constitution of self-esteem and positive identity (Hacker, 1990). As I suggest here, and elsewhere in this book, ethnicity and 'race' need to be seen in the context of specific social fields and in relation to other struggles over economic, cultural and symbolic capital. Essentialisms can obscure those relations at the same time as they undoubtedly provide valuable counter-identifications. We will see further examples of these tensions in later chapters, where I will focus on intersections and interrelations within social fields. Nevertheless, I also believe that the competition for symbolic capital reveals some of the muted modes that convey not only knowledge, but some of the processes by which these modes have been rendered mute, especially in the discourses of social science. This kind of argument has been eloquently put forward by Paul Gilroy in the context of the Black Arts Movement in Britain (see Gilroy, 1988/89). Gilroy also criticises the elision of culture and ethnicity, recognising that 'the Kaleido-scopic formations of "trans-racial" cultural syncretism are growing daily more detailed and more beautiful' (p.37).

I will return to what I call 'the poetics of ethnicity' (including music, dance and other creative work) in later chapters. Here I would like to point out that what Gilroy describes as the 'cruciality of the frog's perspective' – a kind of double vision – is particularly appropriate in the U.S.A., where the population is increasingly non-European in origin. This growing heterogeneity foregrounds issues of 'race', in connection with the large Asian and Hispanic populations as well as the Afro-Americans. But the themes I have traced throughout this chapter remain important for an understanding of social and cultural relations in the United States. The articulation of some of those themes will become clearer in the following outline of some of the work undertaken in the study of migration to and settlement in the United Kingdom.

UNITED KINGDOM

Academic sociology, as developed in the U.S.A., has been widely influential elsewhere in the world. But Marxism was not suppressed to the same degree in Europe and social reformist versions of sociology have remained at the forefront in Britain (see Birnbaum, 1971, for a more detailed account of the establishment of academic sociology in the U.S.A. and Europe). Much of the study of migration and settlement in Britain and Europe is critical – of state policies, of ethnocentrism and racism, of the exploitation of migrant labour and, more generally of structured inequalities. Berger's *A Seventh Man* (1975), which I discuss at length in chapter 3, is an excellent example of such a critical approach. Berger's work has provided part of my own perspective, particularly his views on international labour migration and his linking of structural explanation with people's perceptions of their situation.

More generally, what I wish to do here is to mention some of the tendencies in U.K. studies and suggest possible ways of integrating and complementing them in the light of the framework developed in this book. For the purposes of this discussion, I will refer again to the themes outlined at the beginning of this chapter. The material discussed here, mainly concerned with post-World War Two migrations, contains a strong ongoing theoretical debate between writers described as Marxists, on the one hand, and assimilation and integrationists, on the other (Lever Tracy and Quinlan, 1988) or as political economists versus ethnic and race relations theorists (Miles, 1982). One of the consequences of this debate has been to link empirical evidence with theory in a way that is rarely done in more abstracted empiricist studies. Another consequence has been that the terrain of struggle for material, cultural and symbolic capital has been very clearly defined (although not usually discussed in those terms).

Earlier researchers in Britain, as in the U.S.A., tended to conclude that immigrants would gradually integrate, once language difficulties and other cultural barriers were overcome (cf. Patterson, 1963). But these studies also concentrated on 'ethnic communities' to the relative neglect of wider structural influences on immigrants and the consequent failure to ask the question – 'assimilate to what?' Rex and Tomlinson posed such a question in their study, *Colonial Immigrants in a British City* (1979), where they asked: 'Do immigrants have the same rights as their fellow workers and neighbours? Is group-consciousness and identity still organised on an ethnic basis or by transfer to British groups? Is ethnic identity compatible with equal rights?' (p.14). In attempting to answer these questions, they studied immigrants' jobs (the kind of work, membership of unions), housing and education, revealing that class-based solidarity and mutual aid did not extend to immigrants, and explored the unequal distribution of power and resources. Rex also discussed some of the symbolic significance of the colonial background in the constitution of racism, a historical argument that aptly related the study of ethnic minorities to the longer view of colonialism and international dependency relations.

Miles (1982) criticised Rex's focus on colonial immigrants, arguing that migrants must be seen as entering and taking up positions 'within a set of forces and relations of production', i.e. that one should not assume the primacy of racism and discrimination, but understand migrants as wage labourers, and active subjects occupying a class position in a capitalist mode of production (p.37). Most of the considerable literature about immigrants to Britain is about ex-colonials, who constitute the majority of post-war immigrants. Even the Irish, another large minority, were pre-defined as inferior, as Miles demonstrates, and were subject to further racialisation in Britain (as 'naturally' inclined to violence, stupidity, etc.).

Miles' analysis of racism against the Irish workers does show the importance of a detailed explanation based on political economy, but it provides only a partial explanation of the added intensity of some of the British responses to 'coloured' immigrants. Here, some interrelation of objective and subjective approaches is needed. In a more recent book on the subject of racism, Miles has moved towards such an interrelation, discussing representations of the Other, including discourses about 'Europe', as well as those concerned with 'race' (Miles, 1989). This book brings his work somewhat closer to that of some of the French writers whom I will discuss in chapter 8. Identity and the 'subject', once anathema to Marxist scholars, have also been elegantly discussed by Stuart Hall (1987), in an exploration of migration and narratives of displacement (see further, chapter 4).

In fact, British writers appear to be much readier than their American counterparts to confront the political dimensions of their research and to explore the contours of the increasing racism that accompanied the migration and settlement of 'non-whites'. In general, left-wing analysts have avoided or rejected the concept of ethnicity, while ethnicists have downplayed class relations. Yet ethnicity is an important element in the rhetoric of racist ideologues, such as Enoch Powell in the U.K. (and Jean-Marie Le Pen, in France), who base their objections to immigrants on some notion of a pure British or French nation. Moreover, some groups are singled out for special opprobrium. For example, hostility to people of Afro-Caribbean origin in Britain is often couched in terms of their supposedly unacceptable cultural traits (see Barker, 1981). Since 'race' is culturally constructed, ethnicity is a crucial consideration for any understanding of the alarming and pervasive resurgence of racism in Britain and Europe.

British writers who have engaged with the very thorny political issues surrounding racism have produced thoughtful and innovative work that moves across disciplinary boundaries and includes perspectives from cultural and feminist studies. The collection of papers in *The Empire Strikes Back* (1982), arising out of the work of the Centre for Contemporary Cultural Studies in Birmingham, brings together scholars from a number of disciplines who discuss British capitalism and race, the 'commonsense' roots of racism, critiques of race and ethnic relations sociology, ideologies of black criminality, and black children's experience of educational 'failure'. All of these authors blend structural analyses with closely detailed accounts of the experiences of the people they discuss. They also include two excellent discussions on the intersection of race and class with gender, one of these on black feminism and the other on Asian women in resistance.

Later I will discuss in more detail some of the feminist writing about migrant and 'ethnic' women in the U.K. (for example, Anthias, 1983; Anthias and Yuval-Davis, 1983; Phizacklea, 1983; Parmar, 1989). This work has been part of wider debates – about labour migration, workforce segmentation, feminism and political action, as well as racism and migration policy. They have strongly challenged the prevailing ethnocentrism in women's and workers' movements, and raised crucial questions about structured inequalities and the limits of representation. These feminist studies have covered a number of the themes pursued here – for example, interrelating countries of emigration and immigration, analysing the insertion of immigrants into economic and political structures of the receiving society, recognising the agency of migrants (and its limits), viewing class and gender as cultural constructs, and working towards some combination of subjective and objective moments of analysis.

Morokvasic raised some of these issues in her chapter in a collection of essays on migration and female labour, *One Way Ticket* (Phizacklea, 1983). It may be helpful to look more closely at that chapter as a point of comparison with *From Another Place*. Morokvasic focussed explicitly on women in migration, noting their absence from many British and European studies and the stereotypes imposed upon those who were recognised as present (for example, being defined as dependants, despite a high workforce participation). Studies of migrant women workers, Morokvasic argued, did have the advantage of locating the women economically, but tended to neglect their origins and to assume that 'Westernising' employment would inevitably lead to emancipation. She commented critically on notions of traditional culture, on the emphasis on individual women, and the failure to consider the articulation of class, gender and migrant status. Morokvasic was concerned with sharing and developing multifocal perspectives. Accordingly, she suggested further case studies, especially of emigration, commending Saifullah-Khan's use of social network analysis. Morokvasic also argued that perceptions should be evaluated, along with the socio-economic pressures that surround migration and settlement.

Morokvasic's suggestions reinforce some of the themes I will develop in this book. Chapters 3, 5 and 6 offer a critique of the concept of 'tradition', providing analyses of the transformation and development of cultural processes in relation to economic and political structures and to aspects of symbolic power and competition for cultural capital. These chapters examine the interconnections between countries of origin and countries of immigration, not only in terms of cultural practices, but in the context of gender and class-based relations, in both places. My own interest in these inter-connections developed partly in earlier studies of social networks of Greek-Australians, and of return migration to and emigration from Greece (Bottomley, 1979, 1984b). Chapter 9 integrates the perspectives of class, gender and ethnicity in a brief analysis of 'the limits of necessity' among Greek-Australians, demonstrating some of the effects on people's 'private' lives of state policies and practice, economic change and prejudice and discrimination. That chapter will refer back to my overview of American and British studies, as well as to recent French material, to allow further comparison of the specificities of social, political and cultural contexts.

CULTURES, ETHNICITIES AND SOCIAL POWER

I am particularly concerned here with the relation between culture, ethnicities and social power. These concepts require further discussion, in the light of the preceding sketch of studies of migration and settlement. One of the most pervasive aspects of these studies is the conflation of culture and ethnicity. Culture is rather a polymorphic concept, developed in close association with the concept of nation and the differentiation of ethnic groups, as we saw in chapter 1. However, it is worth repeating my argument for a broader view of culture, as 'constitutive social processes' (following Williams) and as

Both the meanings and values which arise amongst distinctive social groups and classes, on the basis of their given historical conditions and relationships, through which they handle and respond to the conditions of existence; *and* (as) the lived traditions and practices through which those 'understandings' are expressed and in which they are embodied. (Hall, 1981, p.26)

According to this definition, ethnic groups, defined by some real or imagined shared origins, must be seen as part of a range of possible groups or classes, and therefore as responsible for some of the meanings, values, beliefs and practices through which we understand our conditions of existence. But meanings and practices are always contested. There are struggles for symbolic as well as economic capital, and these struggles occur within and between groups and classes. Contested definitions of ethnic identity, as well as practices deemed 'appropriate' to women will be discussed in chapters 5, 6 and 7 below. But we will also see, in those chapters, some of the ramifications of class position in the construction of forms of ethnicity and gender relations. My basic argument is that the three perspectives of class, gender and ethnicity interpenetrate, and that their separation impoverishes our understanding of all three.

Studies in the U.S.A. have often failed to question the constitution of ethnicity, thus neglecting the struggles for symbolic as well as material resources that have marked the formation of their nation of immigrants. Writers who have turned their attention to those struggles have presented a much livelier view of immigration and the politics of culture. The work of Herbert Gutman, for example, explores the development of a culture of industrial capitalism and the pressures required to 'assimilate' rural, pre-industrial workers into this particular cultural mode. These pressures cannot realistically be labelled as 'ethnic', although the heterogeneous oppressed had, in general, different origins from those in command of the pressing. Similarly, the subjects of Sennett and Cobb's book suffered from class-based injuries more than from ethnic oppression. These injuries were related to material deprivation, poverty and exploitation, but also to the cultural forms that accompany status distinctions and deprive people of dignity and self-respect. Under these circumstances, beliefs and practices associated with ethnicity can act as a reminder that one may claim *some* basis for respect. For example, Ricca Kartides, one of their interviewees, made 'heroic efforts of time, work and personal sacrifice' in order to buy a house for his family in Boston. In the live-in apartment where he was employed as a janitor, his children were forbidden to enter by the front door or to play on the empty lawns surrounding the building. Kartides' self-respect as a good Greek father was constantly cut across by the inferior status accorded a janitor in the U.S.A. (but not, Kartides explained, in Greece).

Those American studies that do link class with ethnicity or 'race' in this way also break through two of the dichotomies that beset much of the British material. These are the subjective–objective and culturalist–structuralist dichotomies. I argue here, again following Bourdieu, that both the subjective and objective moments are necessary, but that one cannot deduce actions and interactions from structures nor assume homogeneity of social conditions in apparently unified groups. Clearly, there are objective structures that orient and constrain, but there is also a social genesis of schemes of perception and representation. We see the relation of these two most clearly, perhaps, in the literary work discussed in chapter 4, where material and symbolic structures intersect in biographies and autobiographies. This dialectic is also visible in those ethnographic studies that include both structures and perceptions.

Richard Johnson, arguing against the subjective–objective dichotomy, describes cultural studies as being 'about the historical forms of consciousness or subjectivity' or 'the subjective side of social relations' (1986, p.280). In the same paper, Johnson tackles the opposition between structuralist and culturalist approaches, an opposition he believes to be 'a sure impediment to the development of cultural studies' (1986, p.290). As Johnson acknowledges, feminist research has challenged the usefulness of these dichotomies (and others, such as the public–private). Another strong challenge to boundaries has come from the kind of artistic work discussed by Gilroy as interrogating the very definitions of Western modernity as being premised on the exclusion of the Other, and proposing instead a 'global, populist-modernist perspective' (1988/89, p.42) that looks outward rather than remaining within ethnic or national particularities.

Once again, it seems that the best approach to an understanding of migration and what I have called the politics of culture is by way of asking more general questions – about movements of labour in international capitalism, the development of industrialist and post-industrialist societies, forms of cultural oppression and expression in heterogeneous societies and about what Foucault described as 'mechanisms of subjection', which 'entertain complex and circular relations' with other forms of domination (1982, p.213). The development of separate ethnic, racial or multicultural studies implies that 'ethnics', migration and racism can be studied separately from other areas of social inquiry. My own work over the past 20 years, for example, has frequently been characterised as 'studying Greek-Australians'. While much of the empirical work has been done among Greeks and Greek-Australians, the questions I have been asking have been questions about Australia – and, by comparison, about Britain, the U.S.A. and France – as a nation of immigrants; policies and practices in ethnically diverse societies; cultural transformations and power relations in re-defining ethnicity; transitions from rural to urban life; relations between generations and between women and men; and processes of identity formation (including an interest in mechanisms of subjection and resistance). Concentrating on Greek-speakers has allowed me to 'ground' such questions, to develop a deeper understanding of a particular case of the range of possibilities, rather than to remain at a level of generality. I believe that is one of the most useful elements of an anthropological approach; it requires detailed contextual analyses of social relations and cultural forms.

In this book, I endeavour to travel beyond and across some of the boundaries encountered in sociological work. By moving through large-scale studies of international migration and the historical constructions of cultural differences, to an examination of the politics and poetics of ethnicity, through more closely-grained analyses of cultural practices such as dance and dowry to the interrelation of class and ethnicity with gender and age, I have kept in mind questions that are not limited to one country, one context, one theoretical framework or one academic discipline.

CHAPTER 3

Traditions, structures and culture as process

... cultural sets of practices and ideas (are) put into play by
determinate human actors under determinate circumstances.
In the course of action, these cultural sets are forever
assembled, dismantled and reassembled, conveying in variable
accents the divergent paths of groups and classes.
Wolf, 1982, pp.390–1

In this chapter, I will develop some of the interconnections between migration and culture, keeping in mind the themes introduced in the first two chapters. One of the problems of discussing cultural practices within this context is that students of migration, especially, have tended to assume separate and often opposed perspectives that can loosely be described as either 'culturalist' or 'structuralist' (usually 'Marxist', in the latter case). Ethnicity, as a concept, and culture, by association, have been regarded as the province of the former category. For example, Miles (1982) has carefully analysed 'the ethnic relations problematic' and criticised its emphasis on cultural differentiation as the primary focus of interest. Such an emphasis fails to identify class divisions within the culturally distinct groups or their interconnection with the wider social formation. He argues that it is important to recognise that members of ethnic groups also have positions in production, and therefore class relations (see esp. pp.67–71).

Nevertheless, Miles sees the significance of the ethnic relations model (a) in pointing out that ethnicity, rather than phenotypical characteristics, can be a source of conflict; (b) in seeing migrants as agents and not simply passive victims; and (c) in demonstrating the connections between economic and political conditions in countries of origin and those in immigrant-receiving countries.

Other critics have concentrated on the ways in which an emphasis on ethnicity has obscured class and gender-based inequalities in

36

countries of immigration (see de Lepervanche, 1980; Jakubowicz, 1981, 1983). Some of the ethnicists, on the other hand, have completely ignored class and gender inequalities or regarded them as unproblematic (see ACPEA, 1982).

In fact, variables of ethnicity and gender do complicate a class analysis in a way that has only recently been systematically confronted. To my knowledge, the most successful attempt to theorise this problem has been that made by Floya Anthias and Nira Yuval-Davis in a paper called, 'Contextualising feminism – gender, ethnic and class divisions' published in *Feminist Review* in 1983. The authors, referring mainly to British experience, argue that 'every feminist struggle has a specific ethnic (as well as class) context' (p.62). They note the tendency of Marxists to reduce ethnic and gender divisions to some form of class division, and of feminists to render ethnic, and sometimes class divisions invisible in assuming unitary and biological roots of sisterhood.

All three divisions have an organizational, experiential and representational form, are historically produced and therefore changeable, are affected by and affect each other and the economic, political and ideological relations in which they are inserted. Relations of power are usually found within each division and thus often the existence of dominant and subordinate partners. They are all therefore framed in relation to each other within relations of domination. They may thus involve political mobilization, exclusion from particular resources and struggles over them, claims to political representation and the formation of concrete interests and goals which may shift over time. It is not a question therefore of one being more 'real' than the others or a question of which is the most important . . . it is clear that the three divisions prioritize different spheres of social relations and will have different effects which it may be possible to specify in concrete analysis. However we suggest that each division exists within the context of the others and that any concrete analysis has to take this into account. (1983, p.65)

Anthias (1983) has used this approach in a study of sexual divisions and ethnic adaptation among Greek-Cypriot women in London. She studied the participation of Greek-Cypriot women in the 'ethnic economy', within the British clothing industry. Most of the women worked for Cypriot employers, who exploited their paid labour, while their unpaid labour supported kinship networks and domestic life, where women continued to be subordinate to male authority. Jeannie Martin (1986) has discussed non-Anglophone women in Australia within a similar framework, concentrating on the relation between production and social reproduction. A collection of essays co-edited with Marie de Lepervanche also included all three perspectives, and recently this framework has been extended to an exploration of the intersection of gender, class, ethnicity and culture (see Bottomley and de Lepervanche, 1984; Bottomley et al., 1991). These and related works will be discussed more fully in chapter 9.

Throughout this chapter and the ones that follow, I will develop analyses that seek to interrelate the three perspectives of ethnicity, class and gender, under the general rubric of a politics of culture. Just how relations of domination and subjection are constructed and operate can only be explored in context, but I hope to show some ways in which such contextual analyses can be made.

Here and in the following chapter, we will look at several studies of migration and cultures, then at the notions of tradition and cultural determinism, and finally at what I have called the 'politics and poetics of ethnicity'. Some of these themes will reappear in later chapters, where gender relations will also receive more attention. At any one time, one or other of these three perspectives may have analytical priority, but I want to stress the need to consider their interconnections and not their separateness.

MIGRATION AND CULTURE

As a way into this difficult subject, it might be worth returning to Bourdieu's 'constructivist structuralism' or 'structuralist constructivism', as he describes his critique of the artificial opposition between structures and representations (1987, p.147). Structures that constitute a particular social environment (for example, the material circumstances of a particular class location) produce the external necessity that limits and defines the lives of individuals. To some extent, each of us carries with her the collective history of her group or class, the sense of one's place described by Bourdieu as habitus (see p.10 above). This means that interpersonal relations are never merely individual-to-individual, as subjectivist accounts might suggest. Meaning is produced through categories of perception and appreciation that are themselves social products. The social world therefore appears as a symbolic system that is apparently self-evident.

Nevertheless, Bourdieu warns against the tendency to deduce actions and interactions from structures, and to assume homogeneity of social conditions and the existence of unified groups. There are variations in the limits of necessity and struggles over what he calls symbolic capital, and over the right to impose a legitimate view of the social world.

In the case of migration, this struggle can be seen in an acute form. Migration implies a radical change in objective circumstances. Migrants move into different political and economic systems where they must come to terms with already existing schemes of under-standing and of power relations. Neither a subjective nor an objective account of this encounter is adequate by itself.

Perhaps the most successful attempt to combine the two is the work by John Berger and Jean Mohr, *A Seventh Man* (1975). Berger has always been interested in what he has called 'ways of seeing' and 'another way of telling', the titles of two of his books. *A Seventh Man* contains Berger's words and Mohr's photographs, both making their own statements. Geoff Dyer aptly describes Mohr's photographs as recording the silence of the migrant workers (1986, p.114). The use of poems and the visual structure of the book are themselves 'ways of telling'.

Berger interweaves an account of the personal experience of emigration and migration with statistical and historical information about the stimulus to emigration: the social bases of poverty and the dominance of the metropolitan centres of northern Europe. To quote Berger:

To try to understand the experience of another it is necessary to dismantle the world as seen from one's own place within it, and to reassemble it as seen from his. For example, to understand a given choice another makes, one must face in imagination the lack of choices which may confront and deny him. The well-fed are incapable of understanding the choices of the under-fed. The world has to be dismantled and re-assembled in order to be able to grasp, however clumsily, the experience of another. (1985, pp.92–4)

However, he continues:

To talk of entering the other's subjectivity is misleading. The subjectivity of another does not simply constitute a different interior attitude to the same exterior facts. The constellation of facts, of which he is the centre, is different. (1975, p.94)

Berger's presentation of these constellations of facts is detailed and extensive, but he is ever wary of over-abstraction. The language he uses is metaphorical, what Dyer calls a 'shadow language, a language of alienation that is at home nowhere' (1986, p.113). His homeless, nameless migrant worker is a representative southern European villager who uses his rural experience as a yardstick to evaluate his new experiences. But he is, in a sense, disembodied, in a way that enables Berger to mediate between the worker's perceptions and the statistical and historical abstractions that form that experience.

A Seventh Man was partly financed by the Booker Prize, which Berger won in 1972 for his novel *G*. In his acceptance speech, Berger pointed out that Booker McConnell, who award this prestigious prize annually, had been a major capitalist enterprise in the Caribbean for the last 130 years. In his words,

The modern poverty of the Caribbean is the direct result of this and similar exploitation. One of the consequences of this Caribbean poverty is that hundreds of thousands of West Indians have been forced to come to Britain as migrant workers. Thus my book about migrant workers would be financed from the profits made directly out of them or their relatives and ancestors. (quoted in Dyer, 1986, p.93)

Berger also gave half the £5,000 prize to the London-based Black Panthers, not out of guilt, but as a contribution to the struggle against exploitation and neo-colonialism, as part of his own confrontation with the culture of imperialism that has formed Europeans since the slave trade began.

Inevitably, the award of the Booker Prize, Berger's speech and his disbursement of the money caused outrage and dismay. As Dyer suggests, Berger's work is critical in the sense of 'bringing into crisis' (quoting Barthes, 1986, p.32). Since 1960, Berger has lived in Europe, marginalised by the discursive formation in England which literally has no place for him (Dyer, 1986, p.152). His later work has continued to explore the interrelations of social power and cultural forms.

Berger's association of southern European migrant labour with the Caribbean slave trade is historically appropriate. In his words '. . . the industrial revolution, and the inventions and culture which accompanied it and which created modern Europe, was initially financed by profits from the slave trade. And the fundamental nature of the relationship between Europe and the rest of the world, between black and white, has not changed' (in Dyer, 1986, p.93). The 'guest workers' of his study represent a development of a series of labour migrations that began with plantation slavery. Ironically, most of the southern European countries supplying migrant labour to northern Europe were themselves imperialist powers at some point in their histories. A crucial change in their fortunes came about with the rise of the industrial north. Berger and others argue persuasively that southern Europe has been underdeveloped by the industrial powers in a way that bears comparison to the exploitation accompanying colonialism (cf. Wallerstein, 1974; Schneider and Schneider, 1977; Mouzelis, 1978).

Slavery pre-existed mercantilism, of course, but it has been argued that slavery in the Ancient World did not entail the use of specifically racial categories, as it did in plantation capitalism (cf. Hall, 1980, p.337). Nevertheless, the Romans elaborated legal definitions of slavery that were well used by those who inherited other aspects of Roman law. Slaves were totally owned – commodities bought and sold in markets, whose progeny as well as any other of their products were also owned by their buyers. The Romans justified this status by reference to the 'natural inequality' of certain people (as, for example, in St Augustine's reference to the British as being fit only for slavery). Imperialism had already demonstrated the superiority of the Europeans, whose guns and single-mindedness had enabled them to penetrate far-flung populations in search of gold, silver and spices. From the sixteenth century, Europeans began to transport millions of Africans to work as slaves in the Americas and the Caribbean, cultivating the highly profitable tobacco, cotton and sugar. English heroes such as Sir John Hawkins, Sir Francis Drake and Sir Walter Raleigh were successful slave traders. They carried calico, beads, guns and gin to West Africa, and bought Africans, mainly from Arab traders. Thousands of Africans did not survive the journey, but those who did returned considerable profit.

Berger was right to suggest that plantation slavery has had far-reaching consequences, not only in plantation areas, but in the areas of industrial capitalism. Freed slaves and their descendants provided labour for U.S.A. and European industry and now form sizeable populations in the former capitalist centres.

The next wave of labour migration was that of indentured workers, dispossessed peasants from India and China and, to some extent, Indonesia, recruited to work in the Caribbean, South America, South Africa, Ceylon, Fiji, Malaya and Sumatra. Indentured workers were not bought once and for all, as were slaves, and they were paid at a rate determined by law. But their labour was totally appropriated for a period of 10 years or so, after which time many of them just settled where they were. Obviously, there were different modes of indenture and each requires specific analysis. My intention here is to postulate three major waves of international migration and to sketch some of the cultural concomitants of these.

The third wave, then, is that described by Berger, of so-called voluntary migration, from peasant areas to industrial cities of northern Europe and North America, as well as Australia and South Africa and parts of South America, and to major commercial centres like Singapore and Hong Kong. Most recently, heavy migration has occurred in the Middle East to the oil-rich countries such as Saudi Arabia.

There are considerable variations and complexities within each of these migrations, but they all differ from the earliest forms of migration, where people tended to move in search of food, clothing and shelter (as with the Paleolithic and Neolithic populations) or for purposes of conquest, as did the Huns, Mongols and Goths, and, later, the Greeks, Romans, Arabs and Ottomans. The migrations of modern times, however, entailed massive transfers of population in a relatively short period of time to the centres of economic power.

The development of the wool industry in the European Lowlands and then in England forced agriculturalists off their land to make way for sheep. From the sixteenth to the nineteenth century in Britain, Enclosure Acts and vagrancy laws forced more peasants into the burgeoning industrial cities as labourers. Surpluses were shipped off to North America and Australia. Similar fates befell European peasants, with the eventual consequences for areas of origin so vividly described by Berger in *A Seventh Man*. These migratory movements are often described as voluntary. No doubt some of them were, but the choices were mostly forced by circumstances. Thomas Hardy commented in his novel *Tess of the d'Urbervilles* that what the nineteenth-century economists described as the tendency of the rural population towards the larger towns was really 'the tendency of water to flow uphill when forced by machinery'. In Berger's words, 'to those who have machines, men are given' (1975, p.67).

Having established the centrality of migration in history and especially in modern history, we might ask about the cultural implications of such massive movements. In chapter 1, I stressed the fluidity of cultural forms, despite the association of the modern concept of culture as defining a specific and separate (national) identity. Obviously, with so many people constantly on the move throughout world history, there can be no such thing as a 'pure' culture, let alone a pure 'race'. In fact, Lévi-Strauss has argued that perceived racial differences are the consequences of cultural practices that serve to demarcate one group from another. Rules of marriage, health and hygiene, styles of costumes, the favouring of certain physical types, all leave their marks on the human body. Thus cultural differences pre-figure observed physical differences (1985, pp.3–24).

Certainly, racism cannot be located in the existence of major physical differences, as it often occurs in quite virulent forms where the populations are considerably intermixed. For example, in Australian country towns, local 'whites' often despise supposedly degraded 'half caste' or 'quarter caste' Aboriginal people without ever reflecting on the irony of such a position, or asking the origins of the other half or three quarters! Racisms (as Stuart Hall rightly terms the variety of phenomena) present too broad a topic for my purposes here. However, if we are to consider the cultural consequences of world migrations as I have described them, then racisms are centrally important. The notions of European superiority, and the heritage of colonialism, still permeate our consciousness and continue to form one of the main axes of domination and subordination. Marie de Lepervanche has demonstrated that the concept of race has been broadened to include biological, ethnic, national and cultural distinctions, for example in Australia's *Racial Discrimination Act* of 1975 (de Lepervanche, 1984b, p.50). In Britain and Europe, hostility to immigrants, while often taking a racist form, tends to be couched in nationalist terms, terms of preserving the British, or German or French, way of life against the invasion of alien elements (cf. Barker, 1981; Castles et al., 1986).

The same ideas, therefore, that served to justify the exploitation and dislocation of colonial peoples, including their usefulness as labour in the metropolitan centres, can be reconstructed to justify their exclusion or repatriation. But, to return to Stuart Hall, we must also recognise that racist constructs can be inverted to function as cultures of resistance, as they have been in the Black Power movement (Hall, 1980, p.342).

DOMINATION, RESISTANCE, TRANSFORMATIONS

I mentioned in chapter 1 (p.10) that people 'from another place' often fail to accept without question the taken-for-granted 'realities' presented by those who claim legitimate control of knowledge. In relatively undifferentiated societies, the correspondence between the natural and social worlds may appear as self-evident. Bourdieu calls such a system 'doxic', to distinguish this mode from that of orthodoxy, straightened opinion, and heterodoxy, different opinions (1977, p.164). Bourdieu suggests that even those disadvantaged by these systems, such as women and young people, may recognise their legitimacy, because their only chance of neutralising the system's most negative effects on themselves is 'to submit to them in order to make use of them (in accordance with the logic of the *eminence grise*)' (Bourdieu, 1977, p.165).

But in societies formed by migration and the mixing of people of different origins, and in class-based societies, the legitimacy of the dominant social order can be brought into question. Indeed, women and other 'minorities', including young people, are increasingly questioning former orthodoxies. This questioning is not a purely intellectual activity, but one that arises when everyday experience does not fit the orthodoxy, and the unthinkable can become thinkable. Hans Christian Andersen's story of 'The Emperor's New Clothes' is a simple example. Another was related by Chandra Jayawardena, who described a court case in Guyana where the defendant, a forest-dwelling AmerIndian, burst into peals of uncontrollable laughter every time he looked at the large, bewigged, Afro-Caribbean judge. The case had to be adjourned (pers. comm.).

In much more complicated ways, people who have not learned the appropriate orthodoxy misrecognise, question and resist it, or try to impose an orthodoxy of their own. Even the traumatic experience of the West Africans who were herded into the holds of ships for a crossing of three or four months to the 'New World' was not enough to destroy the cultural forms that constituted them as human beings with a long and distinguished history. Some earlier historians argued that they were stripped of their culture by this transportation and by being sold as individuals rather than in kin-based groups (see Herskovits, 1958). But later work rejects this notion, and describes the considerable impact of West African cultural practices on the countries of immigration. In recent times, this heritage has formed the basis for a lively reworking of Afro-American identity.

Adrian Mayer, talking to Fijian Indians, was given an explanation for their apparent absence of caste distinctions. According to his informants, when the Indians made their long voyage to Fiji, the ship lurched in rough weather and all their food became mixed. Thereafter, their elaborate food distinctions became unworkable (Mayer, 1961).

However appropriate such explanations are, the passage, the movement from one place to another, or one social space to another, can be critical in the sense I mentioned earlier, of bringing into crisis. Again, the consequences of this crisis are very variable and can only be understood in particular socio-historical contexts. Perhaps the most successful attempt to understand the interweaving of migratory and cultural processes can be seen in the work of Chandra Jayawardena, who combined a vast historical perspective with a subtle and imaginative theoretical understanding. His own research was mainly concerned with Indian emigrations, though he was also more generally concerned with forms of inequality in class-based societies. In these studies, he managed to combine analysis of historical and structural elements with more detailed accounts of cultural practices and interpersonal relations. He constantly subjected European social theory to the scrutiny of comparison from non-European experience. His approach demonstrates the great potential of comparative sociology in treating each social situation as a particular case of the possible. As a Sinhalese who was educated in Colombo and London and had worked in the U.S.A., the Caribbean, Australia, Fiji and Indonesia, Chandra Jayawardena was a confirmed internationalist who rarely hesitated to think the unthinkable.

Unlike many of those who argue for and against the concept of ethnicity, or who conflate ethnicity with culture or tradition, Jayawardena recognised that the publicly expressed consciousness described as ethnicity can only be 'understood in terms of particular political, class and status conflicts' (1980, p.430). This consciousness gives form and meaning to the cultures of the descendants of immigrants. But, in the words of Eric Wolf, people 'construct, reconstruct and dismantle cultural materials, in response to identifiable determinants' (1982, p.387).

To demonstrate some of this reconstruction and dismantling, Jayawardena (1980) compared Indians of Guyana and Fiji, who emigrated from the same areas of north-east and southern India and worked as indentured labourers in British colonies, where they were predominantly rural dwellers. In Fiji, Indians were formally designated to a separate status and were not, therefore, pressed to assimilate. As a result, Indians in Fiji have retained and developed a greater and more essential part of the ancestral tradition than have their Guyanese counterparts – for example, retaining both spoken and written Hindi. For rural Guyanese Indians, India had become something of a mythical land, in the sense portrayed by V. S. Naipaul, an Indian Trinidadian, in his novel *An Area of Darkness.*

To me as a child the India that had produced so many of the persons and things around me was featureless, and I thought of the time when the transference was made as a period of darkness, darkness which also extended to the land, as darkness surrounds a hut at evening, though for a little way around the hut there is still light. The light was the area of my experience, in time and place. (Naipaul, 1970, p.30)

In Guyana, Hinduism has a very public face, marked by public temples and ceremonies. In Fiji it is rather unobtrusive, more of a private and familial activity. In Guyana, the Indians were defined in class subjection together with the Afro-Caribbean people, and claimed recognition as something more than coolies on the basis of their ancient and venerable cultural traditions. Outward symbols of differences became important in this competition for symbolic capital.

Jayawardena's complex and subtle analyses demonstrate the inadequacy of viewing cultures as bounded, static entities that are also somehow portable from place to place. His own quotation from Naipaul makes this point neatly:

At an official reception for the former governor of a state someone called across to me, as we sat silently in deep chairs set against the walls of the room, 'How is Indian culture getting on in your part of the world?' (quoted in Jayawardena, 1980, p.430)

In a review of literature about Indian emigrations, Jayawardena put forward a number of variables that should be considered in any attempt at an answer to such a question (1968). These were, in summary form:

• whether emigrants left as individuals or in groups;
• the extent to which they could maintain ties with the homeland;
• their class situation in the new society, as labourers or traders;
• structure and policy of the host society, including the possibility of absorption.

His later work tended to concentrate on the fourth of these variables. He argued:

(It is) the structure, values, interethnic group relations and policies of the host society, though changing in themselves, that have the most constant and pervasive consequences for the social organization of overseas Indian communities and for the persistence and change of Indian institutions in the new environments. (1968, p.449)

These variables were included in my doctoral research, supervised by Chandra Jayawardena. The project was an extensive socio-cultural account of Greek-Australian settlement in Sydney as well as detailed studies of individual Greek-Australians. In questioning the prevailing policy of Anglo-conformity, I sought an understanding of the ways in which abstractions such as 'class', 'nation' and 'culture' can be related to individual trajectories, through a three-way analysis of (a) structures (such as economic, political and social limitations, family forms and ethnic institutions), (b) cultural practices and beliefs and (c) identification by selves and others. The evaluation of identifiably Greek cultural practices, extended from language through kinship forms and religious affiliation to music, dance, food and attitudes to time and to work. As a general guide to cultural practices, I constructed a model from literature (poetry, plays and stories) written about and by Greeks, ethnographies and other studies of Greece and Greek populations, as well as from my own observations and experience of Greeks in Australia, Canada and Greece. This was, then, a composite of observers' models and the models of Greek speakers themselves, which I compared with the more immediate models of the Greek-Australians whom I interviewed.

At the time, I noted several dangers in using models like these (see Bottomley, 1979, pp.78–9). One was the problem of reification, another that of underrating diversity. There is the further complication of the gap between expressed ideals and practices, and the even more intriguing question of cultural modes that may be muted but not necessarily insignificant. I will confront some of these problems in later chapters.

Jayawardena's work and the earlier discussions of cultural processes have shown that cultural practices cannot be abstracted from the political and economic processes that form, limit and transform them. By itself, the most intricate cultural model has the quality of a list of ingredients; in Bourdieu's terms, of a system of durable, transposable 'dispositions'. As we have seen, these dispositions are capable of considerable variation in different circumstances.

Relatively few scholars have undertaken detailed ethnographic studies comparable to those of Jayawardena. Nevertheless, his work has influenced several students of migration who have traced the interconnections between forms of migration, cultural and historical background, socio-economic factors, settlement policies and cultural practices in Australia. One of these was Rina Huber, whose comparative study of Italian settlers in Sydney and in the New South Wales country town of Griffith revealed the extent to which different patterns of settlement – such as agricultural or industrial employment, proximity of kin and of other people from the same region – provided or limited the possibilities for reconstruction or adaptation of valued ways of life. For example, people from Treviso who lived in Griffith and owned farms maintained extended kin ties, including economic co-operation, whereas Trevisani in Sydney, employed as industrial workers, lived in relatively isolated nuclear households and had higher status aspirations for their children (Huber, 1977).

A more complex study was made by Marie de Lepervanche, of Sikhs living in Woolgoolga, northern New South Wales. As well as examining immigration policy, and economic and political factors affecting settlement, de Lepervanche provided a rare insight into racisms and what she described as 'the rhetoric of exclusion' in practice. While tracing the intricacies of religious and local political struggles within the Indian population, the author argued with some force that the status distinctions that set the Indians apart in Woolgoolga arise within the class structure of Australian society. The time, energy and money invested in Sikh affairs is, in her words, 'an alternative to participation in associations of the host' (1984a, p.184).

More recently, another comparative sociologist, Vanda Moraes-Gorecki, has completed a study of Latin-American immigrants in Sydney. Moraes-Gorecki used a gender as well as a class perspective and demonstrated some of the ways in which Latin-American people (a) have been represented by the Australian media (as highly politicised and left-wing, for example) and (b) have organised cultural associations which, while following many of the dictates of Australian multicultural policy, nevertheless perpetuate gender-based inequalities (Gorecki, 1987). Comparable conclusions have been reached by Michael Humphrey (1984), whose work with Muslim Lebanese in Sydney also bears the imprint of Jayawardena's complex analytical framework. In particular, Humphrey reveals the continuing practice of Islamic law and the cultivation of Islamic associations as partly 'a focus for counter-political mobilisation', that is, countering the location of Muslim Lebanese immigrants as a disadvantaged and devalued minority in Australian society.

These studies cannot be discussed in detail here, but they will be recalled in chapters 8 and 9. My point here is that Jayawardena's approach to the study of migration and cultural change has generated research that offers a dynamic view of cultural processes interrelated with economic and political structures within a historical perspective. These studies could well be described as 'structuralist constructivism', to use Bourdieu's term (see p.38 above). They show how specific social circumstances structure categories of perception. They also provide some understanding of cultural forms of resistance to prevailing policies of the receiving society and to representations that arise from the structures of that society. The Sikhs of de Lepervanche's study and the Lebanese of Humphrey's study put considerable energy into the maintenance of religious practices that help to define them as Other (and, in Anglo-Australian terms, as inferior) but they can also thereby claim a moral strength in a heterodox society and, like the Indians of Guyana, some identification with an ancient and venerable history. To some extent, these identifications can buffer the various forms of subjection imposed by those who claim legitimate control of knowledge. People then negotiate cultural materials for some symbolic capital in the absence of other forms of social power.

Australia's official policy of multiculturalism advances a kind of repressive tolerance towards cultural practices of the large immigrant population. But some cultural forms are more acceptable than others; for example, immigrants have been deported or refused citizenship because of left wing political activity. Moreover, the question of representation is a crucial one – whose languages are taught as community languages, and what are the rights of speakers of dialects? What is the usefulness of umbrella terms like 'Lebanese culture' or 'Italian culture', given some of the dynamics and complexities just outlined?

Australian policy makers have been remarkably successful in incorporating the large non-Anglophone population relatively peacefully. The current, or most recent, policy, multiculturalism, basically attaches ethnic 'groups' or 'communities' to the state by means of representatives, usually middle-class men. One could argue that assimilation or integration in Australia means coming to accept cultural forms generated by structures of class and gender, rather than by ethnicity. Immigrant success stories in Australia, as in the U.S.A., are those of the economically successful, some of whom have been named 'Australian of the Year' in various competitions. Anglophone men undoubtedly dominate the power structures, but Anglophone women are badly underrepresented in those same structures. Similarly, the poor are increasingly female.

My main point here is that culture and ethnicity should not be conflated. Class- and gender-based domination also take cultural forms, and it is essential to recognise that much of what is seen as ethnic discrimination must also be seen in terms of class and gender. The struggle for symbolic capital is constant and waged on a number of fronts.

CULTURALISM AND THE CONCEPT OF TRADITION

The reification of culture is one of the shortcomings of the approach sometimes described as 'culturalism', whereby solidified practices may even be seen as determining economic and political forms. In their powerful study, *Culture and Political Economy in Western Sicily*, Jane and Peter Schneider review the cultural determinist writers who explain economic development by reference to cultural codes that ostensibly impede progress – for example, mutual distrust, the perceived inability to organise collectively, or to delay gratification (1977, p.227). Against this kind of determinism, the Schneiders argue that culture 'assists particular groups to claim particular domains' (p.228). Sicilian cultural codes have developed over centuries of dependency. 'If traditional codes persist it is because, nurtured by dominance in the past, they still respond to dominance today' (p.229). Their detailed historical and political study of western Sicily traces the development and perpetuation of the cultural codes of cleverness, honour and friendship, from the time of pre-industrial world systems, through Spanish and Bourbon rule, to the dominance of north Italian and multinational capitalism.

At the end of their book, the Schneiders turn the focus of attention to the cultural codes that are associated with development (and, by definition, with those who advocate cultural change for the 'underdeveloped').

These modern, bureaucratic codes include universalism (fairness and impartiality), individual liberation from kin and community obligations, self-discipline and delayed gratification, and an ideology of merit, attached to individuals rather than families. The codes are 'closely tied to other cherished values such as individual freedom, parliamentary democracy, and the rule of law' (ibid., p.229). They have served as standards of comparison of other cultural forms. But they were developed along with the expropriation of the world's resources over several centuries. 'They are, in short, codes of aggression, rather than defence' (p.230) and they can only gain credibility in a context of continued economic growth. The Schneiders suggest that the rest of the world 'paid dearly for the values that citizens of industrial societies cherish' and that other cultural codes, such as those of the Sicilians, are understandable ways of protecting the little manoeuvrability available to those whose resources have been appropriated. For example, 'to delay gratification in favour of long-range commitments is to run the risk of no gratification at all because colonies, by definition, produce for markets that they do not control' (p.233). To a considerable extent, the maintenance of these codes has been a form of resistance to further centralisation and dependency, rather than a desperate resort to outmoded traditions.

The concept of tradition is a popular one in discussions about migration and ethnicity. But it has also been widely used in development studies, where scholars with an evolutionary bent, including the cultural determinists criticised by the Schneiders, have devised a traditional–modern continuum that carries overtones of nineteenth-century justifications of imperialism. Because, within this framework, cultural forms are seen as somehow free-floating, unattached to economic and political structures, they take on a rigidity that belies the possibility of the kinds of transformation that have become apparent in studies of migration. As we have already seen, traditions can be modified, revived or abandoned if necessary.

Even where people remain firmly in one place, customs and beliefs handed down from generation to generation do not remain unchanged. Bourdieu's discussions of marriage rules, including the tradition of parallel cousin marriage among the Kabyle of Algeria, reveal that rules and practices can vary quite widely. On the basis of his studies of what he calls 'strategies' of alliance, Bourdieu suggests that the language of rule in social sciences is 'often the refuge of ignorance' (1986, p.90). For example, to understand the constraints that organise matrimonial strategies even for one marriage, an ethnographer would have to expend considerable time and energy, whereas a genealogy containing 100 marriages can be drawn up in an afternoon. Moreover, the artificial distancing produced by anthropological studies prevents us (moderns) from comparing our own practices to those of the 'traditionally-minded'. The result is an intellectualism that produces a kind of algebra, whereas, Bourdieu asserts, the real logic of myth or ritual should be seen as a dance or gymnastics. In his words,

Our perceptions and our practices, notably our perceptions of the social world, are guided by practical taxonomies, oppositions between high and low, the masculine (or the virile) and the feminine, etc., and the classifications which these practical taxonomies produce derive their strength from the fact that they are 'practical', that they permit the introduction of just enough logic for the needs of practice, not too much – blurring is often indispensable, especially in negotiations – nor too little, because life would become impossible. (Bourdieu, 1986, p.90, my translation)

Discourses about rules, customs and traditions are considered from a slightly different direction by Michael Herzfeld. In a fascinating exploration of the rhetoric of chastity in rural Greek society (1983), Herzfeld claims that 'the explanation of institutionalised practices and attitudes as "custom" or "tradition" has the performative effect of constituting a standard immune to criticism' (1982, p.162). The frequent claim that women, for example, were traditionally more chaste and that this tradition is in decline, should be 'treated as a primarily rhetorical phenomenon and as an expression of rural identity and morality, rather than as a statement of literal history' (ibid.). Because the ideal of chastity is crucially important, those who appeal to the absolute legitimacy of the past have a considerable stake in the articulation of their history. In such a context,

Ideology, not statistics, is what determines which behaviour characterises the norms and which violates them. By the same token, it is ideology that determines which patterns are remembered as those of 'the' past, and which are dismissed as exceptions that only prove the general moral rule. (1983, pp.162-3)

Such a statement is reminiscent of Bourdieu's finding that the majority of Kabyle marriages did not conform to the official ideal of parallel cousin marriage. Moreover, the same field of kinship relations could be understood through two different readings, male and female, the former, dominant reading privileging patriliny (Bourdieu, 1977, pp.41-2). Similarly, Herzfeld warns against the too-ready acceptance of culturally constructed 'eternal verities' from which actual behaviour seems to deviate. His analysis of the term *gamos*, usually glossed as 'marriage', shows some of the dangers in assuming the apparent immutability of practices signified by such a term. His evidence from Crete reveals ambiguities in the use of the noun *gamos*, including 'wedding', 'celebratory *glendi*', and 'engagement ceremony' in any context where it is clear that the couple will henceforth be able to engage in sexual relations without exciting adverse comment (1983, p.166). The latter usage does not represent official values, especially those of the church, but it is reflected in the association of marriage with copulation. As Herzfeld points out, the verb *gamo* 'shifted semantically from "marry" to "copulate" (and from a formal term to an expression of obscenity)' (1983, p.165). In Herzfeld's words,

The statement that villagers do not engage in sexual relations before *gamos* should thus not be taken to mean, necessarily, that they do not have premarital sex, or that they did not customarily have it in the past. On the contrary, if *gamos* be given the more abstract gloss of 'occasion marking the legitimate start of sexual relations', the statement that there is no sex before *gamos* becomes a mere tautology as far as the normative code is concerned. (1983, p.167)

Herzfeld's analysis demonstrates some of the hazards of what he calls 'semiotic illusion'. But he also enables us to see the ambiguities and flexibility of terms, and their rhetorical use in the articulation of cultural codes.

These examples again raise the question of whose reading of cultural forms is being re-presented. In the case of the Kabyle, Bourdieu makes clear that the male form of genealogies is the official form. The Cretan villagers described by Herzfeld are aware that there are anomalies between local and official values. The Fijian Indians who spoke to Mayer about the relative absence of caste also recognised the gap between their own practices and the codes of Hinduism.

As I argued earlier, any attempt to understand strategies of cultural process must include the perceptions of the actors as well as recognising the structural constraints on those perceptions. Objective relations of power tend to reproduce themselves in relations of symbolic power, but there are always struggles for the power to produce and impose the legitimate view of the world. Hence, the Guyanese Indians resisted definition as 'coolies' by association with an ancient religion, and many Greek-Australian workers have maintained a positive identification as bearers of a long and profound tradition of Hellenism. The force of these constructs is unquestioned.

What can be questioned, as I suggested in chapter 1, is their formulation; the processes by which particular forms are developed, transformed, negotiated, or rejected. These processes are usually political, particularly where they are concerned with the construction of collective identities – what Bourdieu calls the power to make groups (1986). This is one of the important connections between culture and ethnicity. Since the idea of culture has been so firmly associated with national or folk identity, state policies such as multiculturalism define cultures in ethnic terms. But it should be remembered that the other use of 'culture', denoting those who are 'cultivated', is a use defined by class and status. So a concert of folk dances can be multicultural, but an orchestral concert including works by Mozart, Vivaldi and Gluck may be considered highly cultural, but not multicultural. The elision of culture and ethnicity denotes minority status.

PART II
Practising cultures

CHAPTER 4

The politics and poetics of ethnicity

> Stranded between the country you have just left and an
> unknown place where you have not yet truly arrived, you find
> yourself groping in a fleeting reality. But as perception
> becomes more attuned with topological uncertainty, it also
> becomes less acceptant, more inventive and ultimately,
> I believe, more autonomous.
>
> Delaruelle, 1990, p.67

POLITICS

The studies discussed in chapter 3 demonstrate that ethnicity, 'a consciousness of kind', is constructed and reconstituted in relation to specific political and economic circumstances. In this process, particular beliefs and practices are emphasised as boundary markers. Thus, the Guyanese Indians emphasised religion and family values to distinguish themselves from their Afro-Caribbean fellow workers, and most Greek-Australians regard their own loyalty to family as clearly superior to the attitudes of the less familial Anglo-Celts. In other words, ethnicity is used in these contexts as a resource in the struggle for symbolic capital – in particular, to counteract the negative representations of immigrant workers, 'coolies' and those with minimal power in their 'host' societies. At the same time, ethnicity is an important element of psychosocial identity, and the energy expended on the reconstruction and maintenance of beliefs and practices also demonstrates their positive significance, especially in emigrant populations.

In chapters 2 and 3, however, I mentioned several critiques of the concept of ethnicity. Writers have tended to argue for *either* class *or* ethnicity as explanatory variables, and policy makers have often explicitly opted for one or the other as a basis for political organisation. Moreover, the homogenisation involved in the formation of ethnic groups blurs considerable differences within such 'groups' – along the lines of gender, class, region of origin, language, etc. And the cultivation of ethnic consciousness can lead to racism and fervent nationalism. In Britain and France, for example, racism is increasingly couched in ethnic terms; the detested Other is culturally different and therefore deemed to be 'naturally' dangerous, inferior or otherwise objectionable.

This book is intended to present both positive and negative aspects of ethnicity. On the one hand, the idea of symbolic capital points to the value of cultural resources, and a detailed analysis of practices can challenge static notions of tradition and ethnic community that are themselves bases of power (of those who control legitimate knowledge). On the other hand, ethnicity can clearly be used as a means of control and exclusion, and as a way of obscuring disadvantage based on other forms of powerlessness, such as class or gender. Throughout these chapters, I will interrelate objective conditions (economic and political) to subjective experience of those conditions. Hence this chapter includes what I have called the poetics of ethnicity as well as a brief discussion of academic debate about and official policies concerning ethnicity.

As we saw in chapter 3, ethnicity is often reified into a set of static traditions and values which is not further analysed. Questions about whose ethnicity is represented by these traditions and values and how ethnicities are constructed can be dissolved into notions of 'primordial attachments' that 'seem to flow . . . from a sense of natural . . . affinity' (Zubrzycki, 1986, p.9), rather than from social interaction and conflict. This essentialist view of ethnicity can slide into a kind of biologism that eschews analysis of the historical and sociological bases of the imagined community of the ethnos. As Anthony Smith has pointed out, cultural dimensions such as language and religion create powerful ties and act as distinguishing characteristics of ethnic categories, but a sense of community requires a myth of 'a common and unique origin in time and place' (1981, p.66). This claim to uniqueness has resurfaced with a vengeance in eastern Europe in recent years, but the heterogeneity of nation-states is also increasingly apparent in other parts of the world. As Smith demonstrates, it is difficult to establish a clear-cut distinction between ethnicity and nationality, because nations, despite being relatively recent phenomena (see chapter 3 above), were based on a kind of prehistory of ethnic ties and sentiments (1981, p.85).

So, while neither ethnicity nor nationalism can be regarded as 'natural', we do need to recognise that an ethnic base underlies the political formation of nationalisms. This confusion of ethnicity and nationalism creates obvious problems in polyethnic states, where a sense of national unity is usually developed and controlled by a dominant ethnic group. In fact, a strong sense of ethnic community may be generated under conditions of opposition to minority status within a nation. The Greek word *ethnos*, meaning folk or nation, is clearly distinguished from *kratos*, the state, and the Greeks, of course, remain Greek despite affiliation with particular nation-states.

In the definition of ethnicities, specific cultural beliefs and practices appear as distinguishing characteristics or boundary markers or both. In multicultural policies, ethnicities can become co-terminous with these culturally defined boundaries. But policies usually emphasise language and national groupings, using categories such as 'Yugoslavs' and 'Arabic-speakers'. Multiculturalism, which is really polyethnicism, therefore suggests that separate bounded 'cultures' exist, but in practice ethnicities are blurred into pseudo-homogeneities that obscure the constant struggle within and between those classified as ethnic groups. At the same time, only 'ethnic' cultural practices are seen as multicultural. The cultures of the rural poor or the urban vagrants or the very wealthy – or, indeed, those of the various descendants of earlier immigrants (e.g. the Anglo-Celts in Australia) – are not multicultural. As I suggested in chapter 3, ethnicity denotes a particular kind of minority status.

In a lengthy symposium on the topic of ethnicity, a number of well-known scholars, including Talcott Parsons, Orlando Patterson, Ali Mazrui and Daniel Bell, took a broad view of the subject. In their introduction to the published version, Nathan Glazer and Daniel Moynihan claimed that 'nearly one half of the independent countries of the world have been troubled in recent years by some degree of ethnically-inspired dissonance' (1975, p.6). Ethnic groups have been increasingly defined as interest groups. Glazer and Moynihan explained this phenomenon in two ways: the first in terms of the strategic efficacy of ethnicity in making legitimate claims on the resources of the modern state and the second in terms of the social dynamics that lead to such claims and concern the fact and nature of inequality (p.11). Ethnicity, they argued, is also something more than a means of advancing interests. Because of its association with cultural forms such as language, ties of kinship and religious practices, ethnicity has an affective aspect that can be a pre-condition for communal formation. Glazer and Moynihan did not, however, agree with the primordialists' ideas about natural affinities. Instead, they pointed out that many of the groups that have engaged in 'primordial' conflict are themselves recent historical creations and that 'the variety of circumstances that members of a given group can meet in different situations can lead to radically different outcomes' (p.19). We have seen examples of such different outcomes in Jaya-wardena's comparative work.

We have also seen that ethnicity cannot always be understood in voluntarist terms. Ethnicities are imposed, as well as assumed and inherited. A 'consciousness of kind' also includes a consciousness of the Other. Ethnicity can be a resource for mobilisation, but it can also be a stigma and a liability. The upsurge in the politics of ethnicity in the U.S.A. began in the 1960s with the civil rights and Black Power movements, with slogans like 'black is beautiful' and a positive identification with Africa re-defining a negative ethnicity attributed to blacks by white Americans.

A trenchant critic of the 'ethnic myth', Stephen Steinberg, described the later celebration of the new ethnicity by non-black Americans as 'romantic nostalgia'. Immigrant status was equated with poverty and disadvantage and led to negative self-conceptions. In the new search for 'roots', 'lower class strata continued to function as a cultural anchor for their more affluent relatives' (1981, p.53). For many people, Steinberg claimed, 'ethnicity has been reduced to a culinary event' (p.64). Ethnicity, therefore, is not a given, not fixed and unchanging. To understand ethnicity, we must explore its historical and structural foundations. In the U.S.A., the origins of ethnic pluralism were in conquest, slavery and exploitation. Non-English people were aliens, controlled through naturalisation laws and lacking political participation. Indigenous people were charac-terised as 'squalid savages' who could, therefore, be deprived of their land and isolated on reservations. The Mexican Wars also served to provide more exploitable land. The cotton trade, based on slavery, played an important role in export markets in the nineteenth century. To quote Steinberg,

In these various forms of racial domination and exploitation, the nation, under the guise of a racist mythology, had established a precedent not only for tolerating extremes of inequality, but for imparting them with political and moral legitimacy as well. (1981, p.31)

As the South depended on slave labour, the North depended on foreign labour, especially from Europe where industrialisation had displaced populations. American industry was built on foreign labour, inhibiting unionism, encouraging racism.

As I pointed out in chapter 2, Steinberg's analysis is supported by those of other historians, including Gutman (1976), Kolko (1976) and Karabel (1979), who focussed on the centrality of migration to the development of U.S.A. capitalism, and demonstrated the useful-ness of ethnic identification in inhibiting class-based mobilisation. The result has been the development of what Kolko described as 'a nation of lumpenindividualists'. Perhaps ironically, it may be these very individualists who see ethnicity as a refuge, some contact with the communalism of a pre-industrial past. I will return to this point in later discussions.

Steinberg's work showed clearly that ethnicity is not just 'a means for disadvantaged groups to claim a set of rights and privileges which the existing power structures have denied them', as Daniel Bell puts it (1975, p.174). It has also been a means of creating and maintaining disadvantage, and of legitimating inequalities.

This theme has been taken up by Marie de Lepervanche in the Australian context. She examined a discursive move from 'race' to 'ethnicity' as 'a series of ideological transformations in the recreation of hegemony' (1980, p.25). Like Steinberg, she argued that the pro-motion of ethnicity today serves a similar purpose to that of racist ideas and practices a hundred years ago. It 'masks conflicting class interests and the nature of class relations' (p.34). Perhaps because of a slightly ambiguous closing sentence in this paper, de Lepervanche has been criticised for claiming that there are no ethnics, 'only ways of seeing people as ethnics' (cf. Encel, 1981, p.15). In fact, her own research indicates that she is perfectly well aware of communal identifications based on shared language and customs. But her point is that the official promotion of ethnicity must be examined within its political and economic context.

Pluralist proponents of the view that ethnicity can mobilise interest groups tend to ignore the fact that ethnic identifications are more likely to be used to maintain hegemony and oppression. South Africa must be an outstanding example of this process, but it continues to flourish in liberal democracies such as the U.S.A., Australia, the U.K., Canada, etc. Ethnicity as an explanatory variable can also conceal more 'political' bases of conflict, as it does in media coverage and some official explanations of 'interethnic conflicts' in places like Sri Lanka and Fiji. Both situations are much more complicated than the projected picture of primordial rivalries would suggest. For one thing, the Bavadra government in Fiji, deposed by a military coup because of its allegedly pro-Indian policies, would have examined practices of corruption long-established among powerful people, and would have given a greater voice to ordinary working people in Fiji, whatever their ethnic origins.

The Thatcher government in Britain also increased the legitimate use of force partly by reference to increased ethnic violence, such as muggings, resistance to police and 'race riots'. Some of the bases for these problems have been explained in cultural rather than structural terms, as located in the 'pathological' family lives of British Caribbean people, for example (see Hall et al., 1978, and chapter 2 above). A racialisation of politics has developed, whereby cultural differences are accorded a biological and hereditary status that is then used as a justification for continuing exclusionary practices (see Miles, 1988, 1989).

Even in cases of what John Rex describes as 'benign ethnicity' (1986), there are in-built structural limitations and even oppressions. All ethnicities have been imprinted by political and economic factors, perhaps in the development of a sense of national identity, or in occupation by a foreign power, or in the maintenance of a minority status. Ethnicities offer particular readings of constructed collective histories, themselves cross-cut by status and gender and perhaps by other differences, such as religious and political affiliations. The delineation of an ethnic group is a very crude mechanism, adopted, as we have seen, for purposes of policy, but also in the creation of nationalisms.

In countries like Australia, Canada and the U.S.A., where immigration has been a central feature of the formation of the nation, one of the ways in which some ethnicities have been defined is by their official absence. In Australia, for example, despite a policy of multiculturalism, immigration of non-Anglophone people is of marginal interest to historians and most social scientists. In a country where 20% of the current population is foreign born and almost half the population has some non-Anglophone origins, the understanding of immigration and settlement is still marginalised. 'Migrants' may be tacked on to books about Australia as an extra chapter, or studied in tertiary institutions in one or two isolated optional courses. The crucial element of Australian industrialisation, labour migration, is completely absent from most economics courses, and the emphasis in historical studies is on Britain, Australia and their interconnections. 'Australian Studies' rarely include the reality of mass immigrant settlement, and popular representations reinforce stereotypes, such as the Italian greengrocer and the Chinese cook.

This is also a politics of ethnicity: ethnics are devalued minorities, not a central part of the nation. Those who are accorded centrality, as I mentioned earlier, are the economically successful. In a country where the majority of the manufacturing workforce is foreign born and increasing proportions of the country's wealth are foreign-owned, the intense concentration on a British heritage is a matter of some interest. It was particularly marked in 1988, with celebrations of the 1788 arrival of English ships carrying convicts, many of whom were Irish, to establish a penal colony in New South Wales. The particular nationalism being marketed along with the celebrations means little to those who lack enthusiasm for this form of settlement, especially the indigenous people who were dispossessed and subsequently decimated by the colonisers. A possibly positive outcome might be that, because Aboriginal points of view were heard during 1988, they may be included in the construction of a collective history. The 'ethnics', people of non-Anglophone origin, seem to have faded even further, as a policy of mainstreaming replaces multiculturalism. Since crucial services, such as classes in English as a second language, have been cut at the same time, it may reasonably be feared that 'mainstreaming' is a euphemism for the old policy of 'sink or swim'.

Nevertheless, Australia's highly diverse 'ethnic' population has responded energetically to cutbacks in services, and continues to question the prevailing Anglocentrism. The American pluralist model that informs Australian multicultural policy is not quite appropriate to a country where unionism has played a much larger role. Hence class struggle, however attenuated, is recognised, and union membership is high among immigrant workers, despite the fact that the unions are still dominated by Anglophones. The Australian state has also been much more interventionist than that in the U.S.A., taking some responsibility for housing, education and other services for immigrants, even to the extent of the provision of multicultural broadcasting and television, interpreter services and the teaching of community languages in state schools. By comparison with the British and French contexts, Australian immigration has not been predefined by the heritage of colonialism (although black–white relations in Australia have been so defined). There is also a considerable difference in the status of Australia as a receiving society compared with the U.S.A. and Britain. Australia is not a metropolitan centre, but a peripheral industrialised country with a short history of white settlement. Many European immigrants feel superior to Anglo-Australians and react to xenophobia with their own jibes about convict origins and cultural deprivation. Although Anglomorphism is highly institutionalised, therefore, it is also energetically resisted at a number of levels. One of those levels is in what I have called a 'poetics of ethnicity'.

POETICS

In his essay on 'The Right and Wrong Political Uses of Literature', Calvino (1982) suggested that literature is particularly valuable when it

gives a voice to whatever is without a voice, when it gives a name to what as yet has no name, especially to what the language of politics excludes or attempts to exclude. I mean aspects, situations, and languages both of the outer and of the inner world, the tendencies repressed both in individuals and in society. Literature is like an ear that can hear things beyond the understanding of the language of politics; it is like an eye that can see beyond the colour spectrum perceived by politics. (p.98)

One of the problems here is whether and how such messages can be heard, seen and understood by readers. Keeping these questions in mind, I shall later discuss dance and music with the aim of exploring other perspectives on cultural forms (cf. chapter 5 below). This interest in poetics is not a claim to develop a sociology of literature, dance or music, but rather an attempt to hear voices and sounds that have been muted by 'legitimate' ways of knowing.

'Poetics' in this sense, then, is not just confined to literature. Originating in discussion of Ancient Greek drama, poetics has been described by Jakobson, as 'a focus on the message for its own sake' (Herzfeld, 1985, p.11). But Herzfeld develops what he calls a poetics of social interaction, by which people identify the self with larger categories of identity. His study is based on detailed observations of actions and speech, but he also refers to poetry, music and literature.

My concern in this chapter is with poetry and stories written about migration and ethnicity, which, I believe, can reveal a richness of understanding not usually available in sociological studies. They can also link the objective and subjective, and crystallise general experiences in the particularities of their subject matter. I have suggested (chapters 1 and 2 above) that writers like Salman Rushdie, Nadine Gordimer, Patrick White, Italo Calvino and Maxine Hong Kingston offer rich understandings of the politics of culture. Their insights are critical in challenging – bringing into crisis – taken-for-granted frameworks of understanding. Rushdie described this ability as arising from a loss of place, and intrinsically linked to migration. The idea of roots, of 'inhabiting' a common language and social conventions, all these are lost in migration. Yet, 'there have never been so many people who end up elsewhere than they began, whether by choice or by necessity' (Rushdie, 1987, p.63). This movement, he argues, is a kind of metaphor, literally 'a carrying across', in which people are translated and become capable of reinventing the sense of self. More generally, one could argue that rapid change and the destruction of past certainties has made the loss of place a pervasive experience, as some post-modernist writing would suggest (see Lyotard, 1984; Harvey, 1989). I will take up this broader issue in discussing the question of identity in the final two chapters.

In an essay entitled 'Ethnicity and the post-modern arts of memory', Michael Fischer suggests that ethnicity, as 'a deeply rooted component of identity, is often transmitted less through cognitive language and learning (to which sociology has almost entirely restricted itself) than through processes analogous to the dreaming and transference of psychoanalytic encounters' (1986, pp.195–6). Since each of us carries part of a collective identity, explorations of memory can reveal something of that collective. Fischer goes further, to claim that these searches 'also turn out to be powerful critiques of several contemporary rhetorics of domination' (p.198).

Fischer's essay is a highly sophisticated examination of the problem of writing culture. He traces the 'dual tracking' of the ethnic autobiographer, the ethnographer and the cross-cultural scholar, who seek 'in the other clarification for processes in the self' (p.199). As we have already observed, ethnicity is a process of inter-reference between two or more cultural formations. Fischer juxtaposes five sets of autobiographical writings, from Americans of Armenian, Chinese, African, Mexican and AmerIndian backgrounds, but he also evokes writings from his own ethnic tradition to avoid the illusion that he is not present. The result is a revelation of inter-references and multiple realities, where forms of writing also encourage the participation of the reader in the production of meaning, for example, by using fragments or incompleteness to force the reader to make the connections. Fischer sees such techniques as not merely descriptive of how ethnicity is experienced, but, more importantly, as 'an ethical device attempting to activate in the reader a desire for *communitas* with others, while preserving rather than effacing differences' (p.233).

I have neither the ability nor the space to attempt an Australian version of Fischer's tour de force, but his essay suggests several common themes. Despite their relative absence from accounts of Australian literature, immigrants and 'ethnics' in Australia seem to have been productive writers. In a study of Australian-Greek literature, George Kanarakis names 82 writers, including postal workers, factory hands, fishermen, civil servants, radar technicians and physicians, all first-generation immigrants (Kanarakis, 1985). According to one reviewer, 'the obsessive theme' of this writing, is *xenitia*, the experience of exile, and 'the dominant emotion seems to be humiliation' (Bien, 1987, p.122). I will return to this theme of *xenitia* when discussing dance and music (chapter 5 below). Here, it is worth noting that *xenitia* has been a theme in Greek poetry since the fifteenth century, and reappeared with force after the huge migrations of the nineteenth and twentieth centuries, when literally millions emigrated.

One outstanding Greek-Australian poet, Dimitris Tsaloumas, who was 1983 winner of the National Book Council's Award for Australian Literature, rarely writes explicitly about Australia, despite his almost 40 years as an immigrant. Tsaloumas' poetry has been described as 'obstinately Greek', with 'an underlying tone of a sadness of the soul, a regret for a lost past . . . and a distant remembered country' (Grundy, 1983, p.xiv). But his themes are universal, from his 'Observations of a Hypochondriac' and 'Morning Lullaby for a Sick Child' to the eery, satirical 'Green Ants', a brilliant statement about uranium mining and the exploitation of Australia's Aborigines (1983).

In his study of Tsaloumas' work, Con Castan (1990) discusses the theme of *xenitia*, which, he argues, diminishes in the poet's more recent verse, written in English. Despite Tsaloumas' obvious mastery of the English language and deep understanding of literature in English, he wrote in Greek for the first 20 years of his life in Australia. Tsaloumas energetically resists being described as an 'ethnic' writer, and the pressures to represent the hardships of migration. Nevertheless, Castan demonstrates that the loss of place (the important concept of *topos* in Greek) is central to his poetry, 'a constant but un-named presence' (p.139). Moreover, Tsaloumas' ability to write fine poetry in Greek and in English points to what Castan describes as a 'Bakhtin effect', whereby the fully bilingual poet can stand outside the language of his poetry and achieve a quality of interlocution of each language (pp.26–32). The result is an extension of the possibilities of both languages, a truly inter-cultural achievement.

Other writers are more committed to a critique of 'migrantness', of the minority status and exploitation that usually accompanies labour migration and of the consumerism and superficialities of Australian society and culture. Vasso Kalamaras's moving play *The Bread Trap* (1986) and Rosa Cappiello's satirical *Paese Fortunato* (*Lucky Country*) (1981) are examples. A different perspective on Australian politics has also been offered in the songs of Cretan-born George Tsourdalakis, bringing Greek mythic and literary references to bear on events such as the dismissal of the Australian Prime Minister, Gough Whitlam in 1975 (cf. Parkhill, 1983). Linguistic and literary conventions are confronted by some writers who, using the medium of English with the linguistic sensitivity of polyglots, manage to convey the experience of a non-English speaker by means of sentence structure, linguistic forms and even by punctuation. These works can show graphically the centrality of language in the everyday transactions of migrant and minority status. One such writer, Π.O., manages to do this for a whole neighbourhood in Melbourne, Australia (a city often described as the world's third largest Greek city, Melbourne has some 150,000 Greek-Australians). Π.O., himself Greek-born, writes mainly in a kind of Greek-Australian ethnolect, often about Greek-speakers, but also about Anglophones, Vietnamese immigrants and other locals in the inner-city suburb of Fitzroy. Π.O's drawings complement his poetry, which is also graphically presented on the page in ways that emphasise the sounds of words (as in 'wh-------oo?') or their context (as in a poem about billiards that includes the dazzling trajectory of one winning shot). Π.O.'s poetry touches on unemployment, racism, nostalgia and exploitation as everyday realities, but there is neither condescension nor celebration in his work. It is compassionate but humorous and centrally concerned with what I earlier called 'muted modes'.

The following segment of his poem 'Ta!' (an Australian version of 'thanks') shows this highly sophisticated ability to sketch the disjunction between the limits of possibility and someone's expression of bravado in the face of those limits. The poem is about a young man working in a Greek cafe.

> . . .like,
> the other day:
> While i was cleaning-out the frij.
> I heard
> one of the Greek-men say:
> 'Dai letz mi/
> If eye wuntz to'
> . . . so i
> scribbled it
> down: A quick Picasso
> of sorts (cos i
> was busy at the time): 'Dai letz mi/
> If eye wuntz to'
>
> . . . but,
> the more
> I thought about it;
> Turning it
> over + over in my head like
> a Haiku: 'Dai letz mi/
> If eye wuntz to
> the more + more it started to sound
> like bull-
> shit.
>
> I mean:
> I don't think
> Anyone's going to 'letz' him.
> Not with an accent like that.
> No Way!
> That accent's his passport to FORDS
> or GMH
> Not the World
> No Way!
> . . .

II.O., 1989, pp. 12–13.

Another Melbourne-based writer, Nikos Papastergiadis, also concentrates on linguistic forms in writing about the kinds of jobs available to migrant workers. This example comes from his poem 'The New Language':

Me I don't exist I am nothing
They tell me to pack pallets
But me I not stupid
Me I know that really these boxes
These boxes stamped COLES NEW WORLD
Me I am building Walls – GREAT BIG BROWN COLES WALLS
(and later)
Me I don't exist I am nothing
Study Sonny you have a chance
You must be a someone – anything
Yes I exist but only for you!

1986, p.137

Both of these messages, about migrant labour and the need for the second generation to escape, to 'be someone', are echoed by another Greek-Australian writer, George Papaellinas, in a short story about a young man, Australian-born, who works with a group of Greeks in a factory. In a scene that vividly contrasts the dignity and order of the older man's home with the rawness and chaos of the factory, the gang's foreman asks the young man why he is working in such a job. Peter replies,

'I need . . . I need a job,' and he giggled shrilly. 'I need the job,' and his eyes dropped to the carpet.
'I need the job'. He shrugged his shoulders, unsure of what else there was to say.
Nikos brushed his response away with a slow sweep of his arm. Cigarette ash dropped to the carpet.
'Yes, yes . . . but why aren't you studying? You have their language. Instead you want to work like a . . . like some dog . . .'
and he flourished his arms with conviction, 'a dog, like cattle'. (1986, p.60)

The work of many writers encompasses both Australia and the country of origin, thereby broadening both the perspective on migration and the understanding of the reader. One example is Theodore Patrikareas, whose play *They Call Me Antigone* has been made into a film in Australia (*The Promised Woman*). Another of his plays, *My Uncle from Australia*, was successfully performed in Athens, where he and his family now live. Papastergiadis and Papaellinas, both raised in Australia, also include their experiences of Greece in their writings. Yet another Greek-born Australian poet, Yiota Krili-Kevans, has used her considerable literary skills in creating beautiful resource books for the teaching of Modern Greek, including poetry and prose written in Greece and in Australia. Again, this work expands the world of her readers.

It seems to me that there is an interesting difference between most of these writers and those discussed by Fischer (1986). He concentrates, of course, on autobiographies, whereas most of the work I have referred to is not so clearly autobiographical. Rather, the Australian writers are concerned with class and (sometimes) gender oppression as well as ethnicity – offering, I believe, a more sophisticated and often more accurate picture of Australian immigration than that projected by most policy makers and social scientists. In doing this, they can sensitise readers to a wider cultural dynamic and challenge majority discourses with some force.

In a recent essay, 'The migrant dreaming', Glenda Sluga urges that various approaches to 'the tracing of the exile's search for a new order' should be seen as interrelated, even if their emphases are different, 'because the migrant dreaming is created out of and against the existence of an official version in which it is granted no status or social meaning' (Sluga, 1987, p.42). I have already pointed out that the centrality of immigration is not reflected in official versions of Australia and that non-Anglophone writing is marginalised or absent in most accounts of Australian literature.

It is possible, as some writers suggest, that what has been called 'multicultural writing' will be absorbed as a kind of theatrical other to the Anglomorph mode. Such an argument has been put forward by Papastergiadis, who claims:

Dislocated and disassociated from the norm, the migrant's culture is used to consolidate the walls of the boundary. While a widening in the range of legitimacy and recognition has removed some of the stigma of the ghetto, it has also highlighted its powerlessness. The periphery was once marked as a dark area loaded with private symbols and taboo, it has now become a safe public spectacle. (1985, p.96)

But it is also possible that the inter-references to dual or multiple cultural traditions will pose a genuine challenge within countries of immigration. To quote another commentator,

The formation of identity in language and culture, the self's relationship with space and time, the irrevocable separation from childhood and the inevitability of death are perennial problems of art and literature. These are all sharply focused by migration which turns people into expatriates, tied to two places and at home in neither. For migrant writers the sense of not-being-at-home in language and the world is both the problem and the basis of their work. Those who are not at home often seek new forms of expression with an urgency not felt by the comfortable, to whom, however, these forms may still speak. (Judith Brett, 1983, p.141)

CHAPTER 5

Dance, music and relations of power

If I can't dance, I don't want to be part of your revolution.
attributed to Emma Goldman

So far, I have argued, with reference to a number of relevant studies, that people negotiate cultural materials and practices in the struggle for symbolic capital. Yet 'culture' has been either reified – in the emphasis on traditions – or marginalised – as irrelevant or ideological – in a good deal of the migration literature. In fact, as we have seen, culture is both centrally important and constantly in process. But the connections between cultural beliefs and practices and the exercise of social power can only be revealed by detailed and specific analyses.

This chapter will make such an analysis of dance – and, to a lesser extent, music. I will trace a number of themes here: one has to do with the ways in which dance has been represented, the ways in which people have written about and acted on behalf of dancers. Another raises the question of how the dances may represent the social realities of the dancers: I am treating dance itself as a muted mode that may convey some knowledge not articulated in available representations of the social world. In his brilliant book, *Noise: the Political Economy of Music*, Jacques Attali, referring to Brueghel's painting 'Carnival's quarrel with Lent', pleads to be able to 'hear' the Round Dance in the background of the painting.

Five people in a circle. Are they singing? Is there an instrument accompanying them? Is Brueghel announcing this autonomous and tolerant world, at once turned in on itself and in unity? (1985, p.148)

According to Attali, social theory has become crystallised, entrapped, moribund. Himself a political economist of note, Attali urges that we 'must learn to judge a society more by its sounds, by its art, and by its festivities than by its statistics' (1985, p.3).

71

His own efforts in this direction are exhilarating and revealing. He deciphers 'a sound form of knowledge' (p.4), tracing a history of the political economy of music as a succession of 'orders' that have also been prophetic of new orders. My project is more modest, concerned with some of the themes I discussed in the preceding chapters. Is it possible to offer a perspective on cultural practices that escapes their portrayal as products or unchanging traditions, that contains some sense of constitutive social processes and that perhaps reveals some of the conflicts and resistances in cultural production? How can dance (and music) 'speak' to us about abstractions such as ethnicity and identity, about interpersonal relations or the construction of subjectivities?

It is, in fact, quite rare for dance to be discussed in this way, although dance and music are often associated with power relations. In his essay on the Greek theatre, Roland Barthes notes the crucial place of dance as the fulfilment and the release of the total experience of the forms of ancient theatre linked to the cults of Dionysos, cults that were regarded as subversive (1985, p.72). Attali describes thirteenth- and fourteenth-century prohibitions on dancing in churches and 'assemblies of women, for the purpose of dancing and singing' near cemeteries and other sacred places. Anyone performing dances before the churches of the saints could be subjected to three years of penance (p.22). Writing about Greek dance, Alkis Raftis tells us that 'most of what is known about dance during the Byzantine era (fifth to fifteenth centuries) comes from the prohibitions and exhortations of the Orthodox Church' (1987, p.1). During the cultural revolution in China, musicians who would not follow the correct line and continued to play certain traditional instruments were severely punished (Marre and Charlton, 1985). In Chile and in Greece, musicians have been extremely important in movements of resistance to military regimes. Obviously, people continued to dance and to play music despite prohibitions. In Attali's terms, perhaps, those dancing the Round Dance in Brueghel's painting were resisting the inevitability of the supplanting of the pagan Carnival by the Christian Lent (1985, p.148).

It is fair to say that critical theories of culture tend to avoid the subject of dance and those who write about dance generally avoid critical theory. These absences are interesting in themselves. On the one hand, the subject of dance is usually encountered in anthropological works. On the other, the majority of dance studies focus on ballet. I suspect that one common link between these two discourses is that of ethnocentrism – or, more specifically, Eurocentrism – itself, of course, an expression of social power.

My argument here is that dance is a cultural theme of some significance that has been largely silenced in industrialised societies. Even the absence of dance from 'serious' discourse or its limitation to particular contexts, is a form of silencing. Yet it is possible for almost everyone to dance and people continue to dance, even in industrial societies and perhaps even during revolutions. As Emma Goldman implied, there could be something subversive about dance, partly because it communicates from body to body and evades words.

That potential subversion will form one of the themes of this chapter. Much of my evidence will come from the Greeks, for whom dance has been and still is an important cultural practice, despite urbanisation and the growth of industrial capitalism. In her superb study of *Dance and the Body Politic in Northern Greece*, Jane Cowan remarks that, 'in a society where most people dance, dancing is much more than knowing the steps; it involves both social knowledge and social power' (1990, p.xii). Cowan's book explores definitions of the imaginable through dance events which, she argues, 'can be read as an embodied discourse on the moral relations between the individual and some larger collectivity' (p.131). In the celebrations she describes, elements of social inequality and social affiliation are 'bound together on the topography of the body – within an event that is vivid, intoxicating, engrossing' (p.133). Cowan's work is important in its critique of monolithic notions about a shared culture, its emphasis on pluralities, contestations and ambivalence and its demonstration of the social and historical constitution of habitus, the embodiment of communal relations. Her detailed ethnographic work reinforces some of the arguments put forward here, and I will return to Cowan's study in this and later chapters. My intentions here are slightly more general and comparative, concerned with power relations within other forms of dancing, as well, in an attempt to develop some of the ideas already outlined about the politics of culture.

MUSIC, DANCE AND REPRESENTATION

Attali describes three strategic uses of music by power. The first of these was in *ritual*, to make people forget the general violence; the second in *representation*, to make them believe in the harmony of the world. The third, he argues, was/is in *repetition*, to silence and control.

Fetishized as a commodity, music is illustrative of the evolution of our entire society: deritualize a social form, repress an activity of the body, specialize its practice, sell it as a spectacle, generalize its consumption, then see to it that it is stockpiled until it loses its meaning. (Attali, 1985, p.5)

Is it possible to see dance in this way? To some extent, it is, but a historical and comparative study could reveal important differences. Dance and music were, and sometimes still are, inseparably associated with ritual; but this association has not gone unchallenged. As we know, Plato disapproved of dancing and banished it from his Republic. And the Christian churches have issued various prohibitions over the centuries against dancing, especially in connection with ritual.

Nevertheless, village feast days (saints' days) in Greece and elsewhere include religious ritual and dance, as do Easter celebrations, christenings and weddings. Even in relatively non-dancing societies, the association of dance with ritual is still present. In countries like England and France, country dances are being revived, with some degree of ritualisation that deserves and will receive closer scrutiny.

In France and Italy, these social dances were incorporated into court festivities in the fifteenth and sixteenth centuries. By the seventeenth century, specialist performers, adapting the social dances, moved the performances to the stage. The style of dancing of courtly amateurs became the preserve of professionals. At the same time, the gap increased between audience and performers to the point where audiences are now mainly composed of the uninitiated and the untrained; passive spectators watching others perform dances which they themselves can no longer do. In Attali's words, this is a mode of representation, and

the most perfect silence reigned in the concerts of the bourgeoisie, who affirmed thereby their submission to the artificialised spectacle of harmony. (1985, p.47)

This kind of performance contrasts with village dances, or even courtly dances, where spectators could evaluate performances from the perspective of practical critics. Folk dance 'ballets' are now appropriating dance in a similar way, but classical ballet remains a valuable part of the symbolic capital of the bourgeoisie, allowing those who can pay the price the gloss of refinement and the status of patron of high culture.

DANCE AND DOMINATION

In Europe and Asia, royal courts have included dance performance and dance instruction. A well-cultivated European courtier of the sixteenth and seventeenth centuries would have hours of dance lessons each week, and could demonstrate his cultivation by his dancing ability. Processional dances were often hierarchically arranged so that one's status could be clearly defined by one's position in the dance. Couples were incorporated in group dances such as minuets. It has been said that court life in Versailles was regulated like a ballet, with every practice and every gesture choreographed by the most powerful. Those who wanted to be part of court life had to accept the choreography. At the same time, those outside the circle were clearly excluded.

The majority of the French people continued to dance the round dances which regained some status after the Revolution. When the bourgeoisie reappeared, they would dance together with representatives of the new regime in large dance halls. Napoleon placed great importance on dance, and dance masters were again in demand. In 1805, Paris had more than four hundred, who barely coped with the demand for lessons. To some extent, members of the new regime competed with 'persons of quality' by cultivating arts such as dance, drawing and music (see Guilcher, 1969).

In the second half of the nineteenth century in France, couples danced waltzes and polkas, and dance masters no longer trained people how to conduct themselves. The dance masters had withdrawn to the ballet to cultivate the separation of audiences and dancers.

In England, the courts of Henry VIII and Elizabeth I included 'country dances' as well as some lively introductions from Europe. But the style was more and more refined, delineating the cultured from the vulgar. The distinction was apparent in different modes of dancing. The peasant mode included stamping, shuffling movements, often remaining close to the ground. The bourgeois mode was much lighter, daintier, more elevated, in keeping with a higher status requiring symbolic verification (cf. Rust, 1969). It is interesting to compare these modes with ballet, where a great deal of the action takes place in the air.

Frances Rust has traced the history of social dance in England
from the Middle Ages to Victorian times. During most of this period,
it was prestigious to dance well. In Victorian England, however,

to dance with skill and grace was no longer the hallmark of a gentleman:
at its mildest, it was distinctly bad form and at its worst was indicative
of a rake or gigolo. (Rust, 1969, p.128)

The change had come about because of the influence of evangelical
religion and a lack of interest from the court and the ruling classes.
But it was also related to the fact that dancing skill had become
available to 'the masses', so that it was no longer a diacritical feature
of class position. As Rust has noted, *where* one danced became
important, rather than what or how.

In countries like Greece, with rich traditions of rural dance,
performing groups have begun to take over from the people who
used to dance. Accordingly, dances have been routinised, to be taught
in schools by gymnastics teachers, or to be shown to audiences in
city and countryside. The rural traditions of Greece have always been
devalued by the urban bourgeoisie, who generally preferred European
modes. At the court of King Otto, the first king of 'independent'
Greece, and a Bavarian at that, the royal Ball would begin with a
Tsamikos and a *Kalamatianos*, danced by some of the fierce old
warriors who fought for freedom from the Turks, resplendent in their
white kilts and stockings. But this was a token gesture. Once over,
the guests could whirl into their waltzes and mazurkas, dances that
required special instruction and denoted cultivation (European-
ness). I shall return to this point.

In modern Greece, the circle dances are closely identified with the
countryside. Urban people still tend to dance European or American
style, except in those tavernas frequented by rural immigrants from
particular regions.

In eastern Europe, the state has encouraged national folk dance
companies, the best known being the Moiseyev Ballet of the U.S.S.R.,
whose beautiful dances may be a long way from their village origins.
As with classical ballet, these dancers are trained for years, so that
the peasant dance becomes an art form, removed from those who
used to dance something like them in the villages. The rural people
are being represented in these dances, where their cultural practices
become a spectacle, generalised for consumption. The differences
that mark one village from another, or even one dance from another,
are homogenised for the performance. In countries like Australia,

with highly diverse populations, these spectacles are public statements of ethnicity, delineating what Benedict Anderson calls 'imagined communities' (1983).

COMMUNALISM AND CULTURAL HEGEMONY

I have already suggested that dance can be used in the maintenance of cultural hegemony, as part of the definition of who is superior and who is coarse or out of fashion. In fact, my interest in this topic arose when second-generation Greek-Australians told me how their Athens-based kin scoffed at circle dances. Although these kin may have been relatively recent immigrants to the city, their need to distance themselves from their rural origins included a rejection of those dances that have been retained in Australia.

In Greek villages, as in many others, dance has always been a major ritual of solidarity. As I mentioned above, all rituals are still accompanied by dance – weddings, harvests, saints' days, national days. The large circle dances offered participants psychic and physical communication, shared pleasure, perhaps a relief of tension and an expression of joy. The dance defined an in-group, dances varying from one region to another or even one village to another. Certain groups of people, such as the Cretans or the emigrants from the Pontus area of Asia Minor, maintain distinctive dance styles wherever they are, in Greece or in the diaspora. It is generally agreed that only people from these areas can do their dances properly. They also, of course, have quite distinctive music.

Within the village or group, however, there are obviously hier-archies. Those with more money or higher status are more able to pay the musicians and reserve the dance. Where people were too poor to pay musicians, they sometimes sang to accompany their dancing – women often did this for their own dances. There can also be a hierarchy within the dance itself, with higher status people dancing at the front of the line. Campbell (1976) cites a number of examples of disputes over the order of dancing, between men who were competing for status honour. Needless to say, women and children usually came last if they participated in mixed dances.

Despite the communal character of these dances, they could include expressions of hostility to rulers and exploiters. Elsewhere I have described harvesting dances where reapers symbolically attacked the owners of the field with their scythes (Bottomley and Raftis, 1984).

Other examples are not hard to find, although such expressions of hostility and rebellion have often been filtered out of laographers' reports about rural Greece – another way of denying the political realities of popular culture (cf. Damianakos, 1977; Herzfeld, 1982).

To quote Raymond Williams:

Hegemony does not passively exist as a form of dominance. It has continually to be renewed, recreated, defended and modified. It is also continually resisted, limited, altered, challenged by pressures not at all its own. (1977, p.113)

The question of cultural hegemony can be further illustrated with particular reference to modern Greece.

Greek popular culture, developing through ancient and Byzantine traditions, retained its strength during the Turkish occupation (roughly, the mid-fifteenth to mid-nineteenth centuries). The Ottomans did not impose Islam and allowed subject peoples to maintain their ethnic identities, under the control of ethnarchs, with the proviso that things remain peaceful. In a significant way, however, Greeks defined themselves by contrast with the Turks – as Christians, and as people with distinctive customs. Songs and poems show this contrast, and dances and music elaborate important aspects of Greekness: religious rituals, kinship celebrations, even the independence struggle against the Turks. Later, music and dance were integral elements of political activity against the Germans, during the Civil War and during the rule of the junta of 1967–74. In a study of Mikis Theodorakis, George Giannaris (1973) describes the attempts to mould a national culture in Greece, after liberation from the Turks, the European supporters of the independence struggle found 'barbarous and oriental traits' among the actual inhabitants of what they regarded as the cradle of European civilisation. As a result, a somewhat defensive neo-Hellenism developed, encouraging archaeolatry, a worship of the ancient, and a devaluation of the cultural forms that were generated during the centuries of Byzantine and Ottoman rule. The European hegemony was personified in the royal family – non-Greeks placed on the throne by the British, French and Russians. German and Italian music dominated 'high culture', with the help of the Conservatory of Athens, resulting in a consequent disregard for local traditions. The same tendency can be seen in the construction of a puristic language, *katharevousa*, i.e. cleansed of its foreign (especially Turkish) content and closely related in structure to Ancient Greek.

On another level, Greek nationalists who were concerned with the largest demographic element, the peasants, sought to strengthen philhellenism by showing how the ordinary people did retain their ancient heritage. Folklorists, therefore, began to emphasise cultural continuity in defence of their national identity (see Herzfeld, 1982). I have already shown that this process entailed a selective approach to the data, so that certain aspects of everyday life were filtered out, leaving a consensual and co-operative picture of what must often have been a harsh and competitive reality. Traditional songs, however, did record the harshness.

As for dance, European styles were a mark of cultivation, but the 'folk' continued to dance circle dances from their own regions. Gradually, however, the so-called 'pan-Hellenic' dances emerged, especially the *Kalamatanios* and the *Tsamikos*, both of which originated in the southern mainland. Because this was the area first liberated from the Turks, it became symbolic of freedom. The free Greek state became the centre and, as other areas gained independence, people from the 'old Greece' became bureaucrats, teachers, policemen and administrators. In this way, the 'old Greek' dances infiltrated other regions, carrying with them the symbolic significance of freedom. They are always danced on independence day, 25 March, and, as I mentioned earlier, the royal Ball was opened by a display of these two dances. Not surprisingly, they are the most common dances found among Greeks of the diaspora.

It is important to note, however, that borrowed dances are usually altered by the borrowers, despite the homogeneity imposed by the centralisation of dance teaching and the use of some standard 'texts'. In a study of Pontic dance music, Kilpatrick describes the Pontic versions of such exotica as *To Vals* and *To Tango* . . .

The Vals is in 3/4 meter, but the tempo is so fast that it is impossible to do a waltz step. Rather a simplified 'step-touch-hold' pattern prevails. The Tango is much like a fast fox trot or two step and the Mambo is a rather slower two step, sometimes in a box-like pattern. The Bossa Nova, which does have a vaguely Latin feeling, involves hip swinging and a shuffling step which is characterised by an indecisive walking about one's partner to a tune in 4/4 meter. (1980, p.142)

Furthermore, dance partners are not differentiated by gender in these Pontic adaptations. In Kilpatrick's words, 'it looks very strange to a Westerner to see two rugged farmers waltzing each other around the floor . . .' (ibid.)

INTERPERSONAL POLITICS

Dance can also be a potent element in the small politics of everyday life. Large social dances provide opportunities for public display, for lavish spending, for an exhibition of personal skill. High status men are expected to display their success, and there is some competition in payment for dances and monopolising the musicians. It is an expression of appreciation to pay the musicians so that someone else may dance, but it is also common practice to reserve the dance, a practice known as *parangelia*. Under these circumstances, it is not polite for other people to join the dance without invitation. In a Piraeus nightclub in 1973, a virtual massacre was triggered when two plainclothes policemen, who had been hounding an ex-prisoner, deliberately insulted him by intruding into a dance which he had 'given' to his brother (this incident was the theme of a film, *Parangelia*). Jane Cowan (1990) describes several, less lethal, arguments over the ordering of dances by young male guests at wedding celebrations. In achieving their heightened state of sociability (*kefi*), young men can threaten the ongoing collective enterprise of the wedding. Cowan also demonstrates in rich detail some of the ways in which performing bodies celebrate the gendered order, by sensuality, male domination, the appropriation of public space and the condescending treatment of Gypsy musicians. At the same time, the ambivalence about female sexuality as both pleasurable and threatening gains special force in dance events, where bodies are both sensual and controlled.

During my own fieldwork in Greece, I have seen many examples of interpersonal relations being worked out in or carried through into dance, sometimes over the course of several hours. One memorable occasion included several themes. A middle aged council worker had been drinking with his workmates at a taverna owned by relatives of his wife. His son, who worked there as a waiter, became increasingly angry as the four older men ploughed through dozens of bottles of beer during the course of a long afternoon which marked the beginning of their summer break. By early evening, the son was refusing to serve them, paying no attention to their calls for service. His sister arrived and went to sit with her father. The other men left. The father continued to drink, with quiet determination, as his son grimly removed the collection of bottles. Gradually the tables filled with customers and the council worker's wife arrived. A glamorous and lively woman in the Melina Mercouri mould, she owned two houses, rather grandly described as villas, which were usually rented to English tourists. She dressed smartly, flirted a little with her tenants, and often danced an accomplished *Hassapiko* with her son and another waiter or with her son and daughter.

This particular evening, she behaved as usual but clearly shared her son's displeasure with her husband. The tension was apparent, the daughter was trying to act as a kind of ambassador. Her father watched his wife and son with some resentment. Then, quite suddenly, he decided to dance. Moving to the centre of the outdoor dance floor, he danced an expressive and beautiful *Zembekiko*, a solo dance usually danced only by men, and sometimes called the 'Eagle's Dance', because of the posture and movements of the dancer (Petrides, 1975). He turned and dipped with astonishing poise, moving with passionate intensity. He had the floor to himself; everyone preferred to watch. When he had finished, his wife was the first to stand and applaud. He walked back to their table and the tension was gone. As it happens, this taverna was called 'Zorba's' – a name with some mythic significance, as I will argue later.

Male solo dances of this kind are not uncommon, though rarely só well executed. I have seen a young Cretan worker stand up from his table in a small taverna in Heraklion and dance with similar passion before sitting down again, wordlessly. His dance was like a moving sculpture of loneliness. The *Zembekiko* was especially a dance of the sub-proletariat in Piraeus and port towns. By no means a frivolous performance, it can express anguish, sorrow, pain – often a poignant comment on the lives of those who were refugees, immigrants and hounded by the authorities.

Dance can also be a sensual experience, of course, communicating the unspoken. Some dances are clearly provocative, others are supposed to be demure, featuring small steps and downcast eyes – for women. Traditionally, unrelated men and women were not supposed to hold hands. Men would dance first and a child, an old person or married couple would separate the last man from the first woman. Scarves and handkerchiefs might serve the same purpose.

Nevertheless, dances were places to observe likely marriage partners. Dancing skill and vigour, as well as beauty, could influence a potential spouse and his or her family. And the tiresome business of being invited to dance is not a problem with circle dances. Anyone can join the circle for display or enjoyment without having to worry about being a wallflower. Dances can also generate sexual conflict. I have seen men come to blows because one thought another had paid too much attention to his wife. In one of these cases, the two men resolved their hostility by leading the dance together, with the assailant paying the musicians and 'dancing' his opponent.

Dances have always been an integral part of Greek life, accompanying rites of passage, marking significant events, providing a mode of celebration and an opportunity for public display, reinforcing mores and social forms. Wedding celebrations, for example, used to take several days, allowing kin to return to the village for an important ritual of solidarity. At every phase of the celebrations, dances made important symbolic statements, delineating kinship and friendship groups, underlining the significance of property and fertility. For example, Greek Cypriots would 'dance' the nuptial mattress before a wedding – first the basket of wool for filling, then the mattress itself when it was ready for the newlyweds. During this ritual, the mattress was also blessed and a male child was rolled on top of it. Sometimes money and fragrant herbs were included with the filling. In some other regions, women friends of the bride dance the *Proikia* – linen and clothing the bride has been preparing since childhood. Cowan describes the procession of wedding guests who dance the *Proikia* to the house of the groom, and later dance the bride to the church (1990). Even the wedding ceremony includes a kind of dance, as the couple move three times around the altar in the 'Dance of Isaiah'.

At the festivities, dance is as crucial as food and drink, but the order of dancing is important for the first few dances, where niceties of status and place must be observed. On Rhodes, when the women guests had left, the day after the wedding, the men would dance with bride and groom 'ugly' dances (*askima*), i.e. satirical dances with crude gestures. The idea was to make the bride laugh and forget her shyness. The dancers mimicked the way people in other villages or the monks or some other chosen butt of jokes would plant and prepare peppers or beans. They might pretend to plant the crop with their noses or their elbows, plough the soil with their backsides and so on (cf. Raftis, 1987).

In Euboea, the bride's bloodstained nightdress was danced at her father-in-law's house during a celebration of her virginity. Clearly, these dances and other rituals reproduced hierarchies of deference, affirming especially the womanly ideals of industriousness (with the celebration of the *Proikia*) and of purity (with the proof of virginity).

At the same time, the rituals mark her entry into another family, along with her personal property. The particular mode of dancing has also defined femininity as, characteristically, chaste and restrained.

Masculinity, on the other hand, is defined with much more flamboyance. Dance is still an acceptable masculine pastime, especially where it requires strength and agility as well as grace. Some of the most beautiful dancers I have seen were young Cretan soldiers on a night out from the barracks. Men also dance in army camps. Furthermore, dancing is not confined to the young and slender. People of all ages participate and portly older men and women can be astonishingly agile. As I mentioned earlier, the form of these dances frees women from the constraint of being chosen. But other constraints may be present – who pays the musicians, reserves the dance, the order of dancing, and so on. In a Cretan taverna in 1983, I watched a man in his 50s dancing with six women a fairly simple Cretan dance, *Haniotiko*. I was surprised at first that only one woman was actually dancing; the woman who held the hand of the male leader. The other women just walked after them, holding hands. After a few minutes, however, the first woman went to the end of the line and her successor danced with the leader. So it went on until all the women had danced with this man and all could then dance together – very skilfully, in fact. A classically patriarchal procession!

Another interesting question of status concerns the musicians. On the mainland, these are often gypsies; in some areas the word for musicians is *gyfti* (Gypsies) (see Raftis, 1986). It has been suggested to me that Greeks don't like to work as musicians, partly because the job has been identified with Gypsies, and partly because they think it is degrading to have money thrown at them, stuck on their foreheads, down their shirts, etc. The Gypsies have always had a marginal status as pedlars and blacksmiths, often living in camps on the fringes of town and clearly distinguished from the Greeks by a much more colourful dress and lifestyle. They may be skilled musicians, certainly highly appreciated, but they are still outsiders at Greek celebrations. Cowan argues that Gypsy musicians are central to ritual celebrations of identity, and that their very 'difference' helps to define that identity (1990, esp. pp.127–130).

IDENTITY AND DIFFERENCE

As all cultural practices create and recreate separate and distinctive ways of life, so these dances define differences and demarcate boundaries. People in one village will dance differently from those in the next village. As they, the other, can be criticised for dancing 'as though they're treading grapes' or 'like donkeys', We can confirm the basis of our superiority, along with our purer water, prettier girls, etc. This particular game can be played at a number of levels, and it moves dance into what Attali (1985) calls a 'mode of representation'. Representation is even more obvious when national days are celebrated with traditional dancing, and the audience submits to an artificial spectacle of harmony. In Australia, the harmony is orchestrated in multicultural festivals where dance groups represent 'ethnic communities'.

This kind of representation has been criticised for trivialising those who are being represented. Certainly, it implies a kind of power to define, to describe, to act on behalf of someone else. But the critics often miss the elements of resistance and potential subversion that I have been concerned with here. Some Greek-Australians, for example, regard Greek dance as a positive measure of their difference from the dominant Anglomorph population. There is a lurking ethnocentrism in a judgement that music and dance are essentially 'trivial'.

Dance and music are increasingly being specialised as 'entertainment' or 'art' in Greece, but they still retain a cultural centrality. The great novelist, Nikos Kazantzakis, has woven the theme of dance into several of his stories, the most notable example being *The Life and Politics of Alexis Zorba* (published in English as *Zorba the Greek*). The novel provided material for an immensely popular film directed by Cacoyannis, with music by Theodorakis. The Zorba figure has attained something like mythic stature in modern Greece and beyond. In the words of Giannaris, Zorba 'represented to Kazantzakis, Cacoyannis and Mikis (Theodorakis) the ideal man – the primitive, sensual, free, individualist – the Greek male. Millions who had not seen a Greek dance before acquired at least a visual image of Greekness' (1973, p.141). Moreover, the powerful final message of the film was the liberation of the uptight (and Anglicised) rationalist, 'the boss', through dance. As the camera moved back from the dancing figures in that dauntingly beautiful, wild Cretan landscape, those of us trapped in the iron cage of industrial society could identify and also yearn for liberation.

But this 'visual image of Greekness' requires more detailed analysis. First of all, it is an androcentric image which reinforces the heavily patriarchal nature of Greek society; note Zorba's lines:

and as for women, they make fun of me, but I love them. How could I not love them? They are such poor, weak creatures – and they give you all they got. (Soundtrack of *Zorba the Greek*)

Second, it has combined with tourism to trap many Greeks in the role of latter day Zorbas. Edward Said has described Orientalism as 'a style of thought based upon an ontological and epistemological distinction made between "The Orient" and (most of the time) "The Occident"' (1985, p.2). Greece lies on the boundaries of these distinctions, as I will argue in chapter 7. Like 'The Orient', Greece has been the subject of intense interest, representing both the source of and a contrasting image to European civilisation. The peculiar location of Greece as both the cradle of European civilisation and the margins of Europe has been brilliantly analysed by Michael Herzfeld in *Anthropology Through the Looking Glass* (1987).

In the case of tourism, the mythology and often the reality is that the dour northerners descend to the glowing south each summer mainly to enjoy these primitive, sensual, free individualists, to dance and sing and be merry away from their own frigid iron cages. There are all sorts of complexities in this relationship which I have not the space to pursue here. The point I wish to make now is that in tourism, as in 'modernisation' generally, the Greeks are assisting in the reproduction of dependency relations. In its own way, the Zorba ideal might aid that process. It could become a caricature like that of the carefree, dancing West Indians or the watermelon-eating Afro-Americans. The dour northerners do not dance and sing in Frankfurt and Zurich. They make money, import (and increasingly export) southern European workers, dominate the E.E.C. and make vital decisions about the deployment of nuclear missiles and aircraft carriers. The historical reality of Greece is one of the destruction of peasant society and continued exploitation by more industrialised capitalist countries and an indigenous comprador class. The primitive, sensual, free individualist is something of a contradiction under the circumstances, no matter how well he dances.

Despite these grim realities, however, I believe that there are subversive elements that deserve recognition. In my own study of return migration, I found frequent comparisons being made between countries where emigrants worked and Greece, where they could 'live'. Many returned to poorer material conditions for what they considered to be better social conditions and the capacity for enjoyment (Bottomley, 1984c).

The spirit of resistance in Greece is also strong and admirable.
It has been maintained by cultural forms, as I have indicated. In
recent years, especially since the fall of the junta in 1974, there has
been a revival of interest in traditional music and in the *rembetika*
music of the early twentieth century. This was the music that
accompanied the *Zembekiko*, played firstly by immigrants from
Asia Minor and later by urban workers in Piraeus and Athens.
Typically, *rembetika* was performed in small tavernas and coffee
houses, often accompanied by hashish smoking. The songs referred
to prison experiences, the police, migration, love affairs, drugs
and, later, to working class conditions (cf. Damianakos, 1977; Holst,
1975). The revival of *rembetika* has generally taken the form of
listening to songs, rather than dancing. But the *Zembekiko* is still
popular with working class men and women and those who identify
with them.

The question of space deserves closer attention in a discussion like
this. For one thing, it is obvious that the social environment becomes
embodied in people through the relationship between the body and
various structured spaces. Bourdieu has discussed this relationship
in his study of Kabyle houses, and it is also relevant to the delineation
of male and female spaces, both within and outside the house (Friedl,
1976). In Greek villages, some areas are specially designated for
dance. But dance also creates a particular relation between the body
and social space. The Greek dance posture is upright, though not
stiff. Pontic dancers shake their shoulders and trunks, but this is
unusual in Greek dance. As a result, rural people develop a certain
posture. Men who dance have a grace which is striking to someone
from a non-dancing culture. It carries, of course, the assuredness of
Greek androcentrism, but it seems to facilitate sociality. People are
much more at home with their bodies and the parameters of their
movements. As Jane Cowan demonstrates, dance makes people
aware of being and having bodies (see Cowan, 1990). I will return
to this aspect of habitus in chapter 8.

In fact, there is, in Greece, a more general notion of a 'dance of
life' which moves like circle dances, in an anti-clockwise direction.
Thus, du Boulay reported that ritual laments were taken in this
direction, and the waxed thread which is lit when someone dies
must also be wound anti-clockwise, *san choros* (like the dance).
Interestingly, she also recounted the villagers' descriptions of death
as a perpetual non-encounter, where pale figures waft past each

other, not even making eye contact, never laughing or dancing (du Boulay, 1982).

MIGRATION, MODERNISATION AND RESISTANCE

At the 1981 census, 31 per cent of the population of Greece lived in the Athens area. The drain from the countryside has been relatively recent. The population of Athens, for example, was less than 200,000 at the beginning of the twentieth century and exceeded one million by 1939. Between 1951 and 1971, the population actually doubled. By 1971, 53.2 per cent of the Greek population lived in cities (Mouzelis, 1978, p.99). Emigration has also been massive during this century, especially in the 1960s, when about 10 per cent of the total population emigrated. Depopulation and rural decay are pervasive problems, only slightly ameliorated by the return of emigrants and renewed interest in villages among urban dwellers who can return at weekends and during holidays (Bottomley, 1984c).

Some of the rural immigrants have established centres in the cities which maintain their traditions of music and dance. Some groups also organise classes for their children to learn these dances. This is especially true of Pontic and Cretan people. Dances are taught in schools, but with standard texts usually written by gymnastics teachers (see Raftis, 1986). Increasingly, the emphasis is on display rather than participation, that is, on performances by trained groups to passive audiences. The PASOK government has attempted to stimulate local traditions, encouraging regional festivals and performers. But the process of expropriation is well under way as the recreation of culture moves from the village to the state or its agents, for purposes of display rather than the ritual-related practices I have described. It has not yet reached the condition described by Attali as 'representation', of 'a monologue of specialists competing in front of consumers' (1985, p.47).

Attali's next stage, repetition, has appeared in the mushrooming of discos in tourist resorts and cities, absorbing many of the young people into a more Western and hence more glamorous alternative form of dancing. Disco dancing is the epitome of isolation, where the volume of the music and the strobe lighting ensure that communication is narrowly circumscribed. Nevertheless, young people are free of the constraints of the oldies, and this can be a particularly powerful lure for people with a kinship structure like that of the Greeks. The constraints of kinship obligations can blend with a critique of the old fashioned ways of the parental generation. In diaspora settlements, such criticisms are compounded by an unwillingness to identify with activities defined as 'ethnic'. The Greek-Australian writer, Angelo Loukakis, has written an informative short story about second-generation rejection of a brotherhood dance, that is, a 'Greek' dance (Loukakis, 1981).

In Greece and in Australia, regional dances are still performed at brotherhood gatherings and by dance groups from particular areas. Some Australian groups have created heavily choreographed dances for television and other paid performances. More and more, 'ethnic' dance has become a symbol of multiculturalism, in what one critic describes as 'the eternal repetition of the colorfully costumed singing dancing migrant' (Gunew, 1983, p. 18). As I argued earlier, this kind of typology contains and conceals important truths about domination, identity and the reconstruction of cultural forms (see also Bottomley, 1987). Greek children in Australia often learn hybrid dances such as 'the Zorba', and Greek dances are sometimes taught to non-Greeks by non-Greeks who pay little attention, or may not know, the details of style and origin. What people learn are 'the steps'.

It may be a comment on policies such as multiculturalism that they direct attention towards some aspects of the form and distract us from the logic of cultural practices. As I argued at the beginning of this chapter and in previous chapters, studies of cultural practices have also shown a preoccupation with form and with products rather than process. My discussion, however, has demonstrated some of the interrelations between dance and other social processes, including relations of domination and subordination. If dance tends to be prohibited or firmly controlled by authoritarians everywhere, its relative neglect by sociology also raises questions about the limits of our own discourse. In the context of migration studies, the relegation of dance and music to the realm of 'folklore' could signal a form of closure in the definition of 'hierarchies of relevance'. The folkloric aspect is pervasive, but dance and music can also offer forms of resistance and a sense of collectivism. Collectivism is literally embodied in the form of 'round' dances (which are not usually round, but semi-circular) and, particularly, in their shared code of communication.

CHAPTER 6

Re-negotiating 'tradition': the case of dowry

Matrimonial strategies cannot be dissociated from the set of
strategies – I am thinking for instance of strategies of fertility,
of educative strategies as . . . cultural investment or of
economic strategies such as investing or saving money, etc. –
through which the family aims to reproduce itself
biologically and, above all, *socially* . . .

Bourdieu, 1990, p.68

We have seen that cultural practices are inseparable from the
political and economic processes that form, limit and transform
them. Nevertheless, the most intricate cultural model can have the
quality of a relatively fixed and enduring list of ingredients. The
work of the Schneiders in Sicily and of Herzfeld in Greece has
suggested that the concept of tradition, implied in such models,
requires careful analysis. As Herzfeld demonstrated (see chapter 2
above), there can be ambiguities in supposedly fixed referents, and
people re-work 'traditions' in relation to changed circumstances. In
the politics of culture, 'customs' can become strategies in the struggle
for symbolic and material resources. In this process, particular forms
of religious practice, kinship – even language, music and dance –
can become boundary markers. A list of 'cultural traits' conveys none
of these social dynamics, yet such lists abound in migration studies,
reinforcing a static notion of culture as a series of distinct attributes
defining ethnicity. The interplay between economic, social and
political factors on the one hand and cultural practices on the other
can only be grasped by attention to the interplay itself.

It is also important to have some understanding of similar interactions in the country where those cultural traditions have been
developed. This kind of comparison can be a useful antidote to
reification; revealing, for example, that many changes attributed to
migration may also be occurring 'at home'. Moreover, it can offer

clues as to why and how specific changes occur differently in either place. For example, chapter 5 contained information about the effects of urbanisation and 'modernisation' in Greece that included inter-generational tensions, some rejection of the old ways and increasing influence of ideas derived from films, television and contact with non-Greeks. All these elements are also significant in countries of immigration such as Australia, and the comparisons that can be made clarify specificities. In other words, this approach can provide some answers to the question posed at the beginning of this book about the interrelations between circumstances and practices (see chapter 1 above).

In this chapter, I will concentrate on one set of practices, known as 'dowry', by relating it to wider economic, ideological and politico-legal structures in Greece and among Greek-Australians. Dowry is an important ingredient in Mediterranean kinship. It is a pre-mortem inheritance given to women at marriage as their part of the transfer of familial property. It links the woman and hence her family with desirable affines, but it also gives some weight to the bride's family in the balance of rights and obligations surrounding marriage. Dowry, therefore, effects a reorganisation of resources and an investment by the bride's family of origin in her family of procreation. It is a crucial part of the struggle for resources. In some cases, this is a struggle for survival; in others, it is part of a competition for status, wealth and power, including symbolic power.

In teasing out some of the elements of this struggle, I will examine some of the ambiguities in the practice of dowry and argue that its persistence cannot be explained in purely cultural terms, but must be seen as articulating with the accumulation and conservation of material and symbolic capital in Australia and in Greece.

CHANGES TO THE DOWRY IN GREECE

In theory, if not in practice, dowry has been officially abolished in Greece. In December 1982, the PASOK government passed a new family law that included equality of decision making between spouses, divorce on the basis of mutual consent and the abolition of dowry. Opposition to the dowry had been voiced for many years by feminists and others who argued that it reduced women to the status of merchandise and created additional hardship for poor families (see Nikolaidou, 1979; Roussou, 1985; Sant Cassia, 1985).

Accordingly, many families had resisted the practice and now have their objections legitimated. But evidence suggests that the practice continues and may do so for some time (cf. Piault, 1985). Moreover, it exists in Australia, where it is neither customary nor institutionalised. Legal abolition, therefore, is a significant statement, but not a proscription. Nevertheless, it does complicate my discussion, and provides some evidence for Herzfeld's concern for semiotics. For example, in one recent study, educated urban women would not discuss the dowry with a researcher on the grounds that it no longer existed (Shapiro, 1985). As will be seen, I found similar responses in Australia. Under the circumstances, I will not speculate about the extent to which dowry practices still exist in Greece, but will confine myself to a sketchy outline of observed changes to the practice over the last twenty or thirty years, bearing in mind that the majority of Greek-Australians emigrated in the 1950s and 1960s. It should also be remembered that Greece is a country of considerable regional diversity, so that one cannot speak of practices *throughout* Greece.

Especially since the 1950s, as the figures in chapter 5 indicated, rural Greece has been depopulated by emigration to the cities and abroad and industrial capitalism has made inroads into all parts of the country. Moral certainties have been disrupted, to be replaced by more materialist and certainly more confused frameworks for evaluating honour and success. At the same time, the form of the dowry has altered, partly because rural land reduced in value and partly because younger country people no longer wished to live in the villages. It seems that girls especially rebelled against the hardships their mothers and grandmothers had endured. As a result, the customary dowry of rural land and dwelling has been transformed into an urban dwelling or cash payment for the couple to establish themselves in a city.

During this period, the dowry was defined in the Civil Code as 'the property which the wife or some other person acting on her behalf gives to the husband in order to relieve the burdens of the household'. (article 1406, *Civil Code*, 1940)

It usually took the form of land or livestock, negotiated in 'a kind of ritualised contest' between the woman's kinsmen and her prospective affines (see Friedl, 1962, p.56). The honour of both families was invested in the debate over dowry, and it also symbolised the continuing association of a bride's family with her subsequent offspring.

In more recent times, this complex interrelationship of economic,

ideological, sexual and political forces has changed as the society
has changed. Materially, the principal components of most dowries
are now urban real estate and cash. At the same time, grooms, and
especially urban grooms, have been asking for and receiving larger
and larger dowries. Allen explains this in terms of the need for vital
resources (money and housing) which cannot wait for post-mortem
male inheritance and cannot any longer be filled by the usufruct
arrangements often granted to sons while they waited for their own
inheritances (1979, p.145). The result is that rural families may go
into debt to 'pay for' an urban husband. The family may gain
prestige as a result, and there are advantages to having urban
relatives. But the cross-cutting affinal ties within villages and regions
are cut or attenuated in this process and rural resources are, once
again, being fed into the giant maws of the city. Problems of uneven
development and rural underdevelopment in Greece are increased
correspondingly. According to another commentator (McNeill,
1978), kinship ties may also be broken, as the young couple seek
to establish themselves as city dwellers and discourage contact with
their rural kin. Rural origins are a source of some ambivalence in
Greece, as will be seen in chapter 7.

These changes in the dowry system have had several observable
consequences. They have contributed to immigration and depopulation, as rural people leave their villages to add to their family's
earnings by working in a city or abroad. Some women have emigrated in the hope of saving their own dowries or even avoiding a
dowry payment altogether, in another country. Dowry has also encouraged saving among rural people, where expenditure on improve-
ment programs might have been more productive. In many cases,
this saving has meant prolonged debt. Where money has been spent,
it has been channelled into urban real estate, a highly unproductive
process which has resulted in a glut of urban dwellings in Athens.

There have been other serious consequences of the escalation in
dowry payments. Some of these can be summarised as excessive
pressure on families with daughters. In the words of one Greek
sociologist, 'obsessive thoughts on the necessity of acquiring a dowry
at all costs still embitter the lives of the Greek young women who
come from propertyless families' (Lambiri-Dimaki, 1972, p.96).

This kind of pressure led to increasing opposition to the dowry, on
the grounds that it perpetuated the view of women as a burden and
encouraged a materialistic evaluation of prospective brides. Dowry

was based on a legal definition of women as minors who had to be passed from the care of fathers and brothers to the care of husbands, and required material support in the transfer. This definition completely ignored the domestic mode of production and women's productive labour, as well as the reality of a situation where large numbers of women were employed in wage labour. In fact, many of these employed women have been contributing to their own or their daughters' dowries (cf. Nikolaidou, 1979).

In terms of male–female relations, it appears as though many urban men are still making excessive demands and having them met by families in search of a desirable son-in-law. Also, being married is still crucially important to most Greek women; only a privileged few could even contemplate with equanimity life without marriage. Many Greek women do not marry, of course, but an unmarried woman has an uneasy status, in no way comparable to an unmarried man. Men, on the other hand, are far less willing to marry. In the words of Lambiri-Dimaki, 'it requires strong bait to lure men into marriage' (1972, p.81). As a long-term observer, I would also suggest that greater sexual freedom and the increase in tourism in Greece have made the sexual convenience of marriage less attractive to men. At the same time, Greek women must compete sexually with the foreign women who carry with them the glamour of the industrialised core countries. Despite the increasing emancipation of Greek women, especially in the cities, their structural circumstances vis-à-vis men are not necessarily improving at the same rate.

It has been argued that a dowry gives women some footing within a marriage, providing economic leverage and a material base for self-respect. This was undoubtedly so where the dowry included productive agricultural land, but the argument weakens in the modern urban conditions, especially where the dowry is paid in cash. The Civil Code forbade alienation of dowry property, therefore a husband could not sell it without his wife's permission. But he could collect rent from it and expenditures of cash are difficult to trace. Furthermore, as Allen points out, a dowry consisting mainly of domestic real estate reinforces a wife's identification with the subordinate domestic role and cannot compete with the family's main source of support, the husband's income, wages or salary (Allen, 1979, p.151). I will discuss this point in more detail later, when considering the Australian material.

In Greece, then, the dowry has now been legally abolished. Allen suggests that such legislation follows the dowry's decline in importance (1979). But laws do not necessarily follow general social change; at times they direct change, at other times they may reflect the ideas of a minority. And there is always a complex and fascinating chasm between legal formulations and social practices. Those who advocated the abolition of dowry believe that it has been an important ideological move which will also relieve thousands of families from the kind of pressures I have described. There was widespread support in Greece for the abolition of dowry payments.

Whether or not people have now ceased to expect and provide dowries is, however, a separate question. The institution of dowry lies at the intersection of such powerful factors as honour, gender relations, social mobility, marriage and kinship – and, I would argue, the class structure and even the philosophical basis of the societies in which it exists. As a mode of establishing one's offspring, it is intricately locked into economic, political and legal systems. I shall explain these assertions more fully in the discussion that follows.

GREEKS IN AUSTRALIA

Having briefly surveyed the changes and opposition to dowry in Greece, I want to shift the focus to Australian-Greeks, that is, those Greek-born people who have migrated to Australia, and their offspring. The Greek settlement in Australia began in the nineteenth century and Australia is now the home of some 200,000 Greek-born people. It is a diverse population, including Greeks from Egypt and Asia Minor as well as from Greece itself. The first settlers came mainly from islands and coastal areas, and the more recent immigrants from the mainland, especially northern Greece. There are marked differences in such a population, in terms of beliefs and practices, political affiliations and class position in Australia. In general, the earlier settlers tended to run their own businesses, while the post-1947 settlers were more likely to be wage labourers, production or process workers. The large influx of Greeks in the 1950s and 1960s fuelled the growth of manufacturing industries. Correspondingly, they have suffered heavily from unemployment in the economic slump since the mid-70s.

In this discussion, I will be mainly concerned with the population of older settlers, largely because I have done most of my fieldwork among the second-generation offspring of these settlers (see Bottomley,

1979, 1980, 1983). Since many of them have been materially successful, they also serve as the best examples of the process of accumulation
and maintenance of resources which is central to my argument.

In the British-Australian legal and social systems, dowry is neither
customary nor institutionalised. Furthermore, male–female equality
is a basic element of the legal system, at least in theory. Australian
matrimonial property law, in the tradition of British common law,
constitutes women as equal but separate partners in marriage
households. In the settlement of property claims at divorce, the
Family Law Act (1975) takes into account the contribution 'in kind'
of a homemaker to the matrimonial property. Thus, women who
do not make a financial contribution are regarded in law as
productive workers within the family unit. This legal framework
clearly differs from the pre-1982 Greek legal form of *patria potestas*
and the categorisation of women as legal minors. Women in
Australia have more formal freedom than women in Greece. They
can make contracts, assume responsibility and conduct themselves
much more independently than can women in Greece. The idea,
if not the reality, of an independent woman is pervasive in Australia.

Under the circumstances, it may seem surprising that dowry has
not disappeared among Greeks in Australia. In fact, a form of dowry
has been maintained by some people and appears to be thriving.
It may or may not be referred to as dowry, but it has much the same
functions as the dowry in contemporary Greece. I will argue that
this is not just an indication of ethnic conservatism. It is an
adaptation to Australian class structures and to the possibilities
offered by a legal system developed around those structures.

Traditional marriage patterns are often strongly criticised by
Greek-Australians. Nevertheless, they have the highest rate of in-
marriage of any ethnic group, and spouses are usually chosen from
a narrow range of candidates. Participation in extensive kin and
social networks, a proliferation of organisations such as regional and
church-based associations maximise the possibility of falling in love
with someone who will also fulfil the requirements of a similar
ethnic background, a shared religion and an equivalent socio-
economic status. People introduce their friends to their cousins and
vice versa. Some second-generation organisations were founded with
the aim of bringing together suitable marriage partners. Perhaps
even more than in Greece, there is an emphasis on marriage. The
prevailing ideology about marriage partners is romantic, that one

should marry for love, and not for the more practical reasons usually found in pre-industrial societies, but the idea of an arranged marriage is widely rejected.

Similarly, the dowry comes in for criticism. It has been described to me, by a young Greek-Australian bachelor, as a 'degenerate and pernicious custom'. Nevertheless, it is not uncommon for a bride to bring to her marriage a house or a substantial down-payment as a gift from her parents. Furthermore, there is evidence that many men of marriageable age will expect such a contribution. In 1971, a young Greek-Australian lawyer gave me a 'sliding scale' of expectations. According to him, a medical specialist or barrister might cost $20,000, a doctor or solicitor perhaps $15,000 and an accountant or pharmacist slightly less. Inflation would now have trebled these rates. Another Greek lawyer told me in 1982 that his mother's brother was prepared to pay up to $30,000 to marry off each of his three daughters. In his experience, it was common for the bride's parents to pay $10–15,000 towards the cost of a house which is then a joint purchase. The money could also be used to set the son-in-law up in a professional practice. I have other examples of gifts of houses or apartments (known as 'home units' in Australia) to women who have not yet married, as possible rent-earning investments.

According to another Greek lawyer in Sydney, it is 'more usual than not for a bride's father to give the couple some money'. He also believes that young men of marriageable age tend to be 'mercenary'. In his words, 'most Greeks expect something quite substantial and parents consider it an obligation to their daughters'. Inevitably, in Australia as in Greece, one hears stories about women being abandoned in favour of another with a bigger dowry. The critiques of materialist evaluations of women which I mentioned earlier, are obviously relevant to Australia as well as to Greece.

It is difficult to verify the extent of these practices in Australia. There is no dowry contract, and the exchange of gifts is a private matter. But the everpresent gossip network is an important source of information because honour and prestige are generated and evaluated by gossip. The Greek population in Australia is relatively closely knit, partly because most Greeks came through the process of chain migration (that is, one person sponsored another who sponsored another and so on). As a result, large and dense networks have developed and there is considerable overlapping of social groups. In such a social environment, members are highly visible and reputation important. For some, this closeness can be oppressive, but it can also create what I have called a 'moral community' within which the performance of others can be evaluated.

Prestige will accrue, therefore, to the parents who can provide large dowries. They show their own success in this way, and let it be known just how big the dowry was. On the other hand, some resentment can be generated among those who feel they have not fared well in the bargaining. For example, one of my informants, who did not receive as large a dowry as his wife's sister's husband, resents the fact that their father-in-law implies to outsiders that there was equal payment. In such a case, the father-in-law's prestige is being increased at the expense of his son-in-law, who feels that he has not received due credit for his own achievement in establishing his family of procreation.

It is often the case that parents feel an obligation to provide a dowry because they are still surrounded by this moral community with its traditional expectations of behaviour defined as honourable. In Australia as in Greece, many families without much money work very hard to provide for their daughters. In Sydney as in Athens, women may work in factories partly for the sake of their daughters' dowries.

Whether or not she has a dowry, a Greek girl will initially have a large trousseau, with innumerable sheets, towels, pillowslips, night-dresses and so on. In 1971, I attended a pre-wedding 'bed-making' celebration (*to krevvati*) where the 17-year-old bride, whose parents were factory workers, had 23 nightdresses, 14 negligées, 12 pairs of sheets and pillowslips, 3 dozen towels, 3 dinner sets, dozens of glasses and enough kitchen equipment to open a restaurant. The bride herself had never been a wage-earner, but married straight from school. Her parents also gave the couple a trip to Greece as a wedding present.

One could ask, at this point, just how Greek are these traditions. Anglo-Australian girls also accumulate trousseaux, but rarely on such a scale. And I have not heard of their mothers working just to save for daughters' weddings. The display element of a wedding is quite general; people of all nationalities may spend large sums on lavish weddings, and even go into debt to do so. It is also likely that the large wedding gifts I have discussed are widespread among those who can afford such expenditures. It is difficult to compare, because the evidence is so private. I would suggest, however, that Greeks have adapted the dowry tradition to the existing Australian practices of keeping resources within the family. And, of course, the more resources the family has, the more complex are the procedures of retention. What I am arguing is that gifts of large sums of money or real estate (or both) are related to social mobility and the maintenance of class position rather than to the retention of any specifically Greek traditions.

Greek familism has undoubtedly been useful in this process. Materially successful immigrants have often run family businesses, where resources and work were shared. Honour and prestige still adhere to families, and presentations have symbolic as well as material value. Those settlers who established businesses in Australia were less obliged to alter the structures of kinship and family organisation that had developed in a rural setting in Greece. The family could still operate as something like a unit of production, with family members working for the family business, and a constant overlapping of the economic and domestic spheres of life. This is partly why these settlers have been so successful; the family could make a common effort and pool resources of labour and capital. Some also made high profit investments such as real estate. To some extent, the large gifts I have been discussing will buy prestige with this accumulated money. At the same time, they have been able to utilise the process by which the bourgeoisie have historically extended status and privilege. The Australian economic system, of course, is structured to facilitate this process, with its family companies, family trusts and various hedges against inflation, for those with the capital to build hedges.

In fact, familism can be extremely valuable in industrial capitalism, despite much of the writing about industrial societies suggesting an inevitable narrowing of kinship obligations and a corresponding demise of kinship. While it is true that industrial capitalism frag-ments individual workers and alienates people from each other, it is also true that the most successful capitalists have 'made it' as a family. One has only to think of the Rothschilds, the Kennedys, the Roosevelts, the Rockefellers, the Vesteys and so on, not to mention the House of Windsor. Furthermore, industrial capitalism is so structured as to favour accumulation by families. Not only can bourgeois families ensure for their children a certain kind of education and access to influential networks (cultural capital), they can also pass on hard cash, usually with impunity. They can establish family trusts and register family companies, thus utilising tax deductions and concessions to stretch the family income much further than any wage earner could manage. These large gifts, for example, are free of gift tax and reduce interest bearing savings for the donors. At the same time, they provide valuable assets for a newly-married couple, either for a dwelling or towards the cost of a professional practice. Obviously, this assistance enables the socially mobile to establish their offspring firmly in the higher reaches of the social scale.

The form of dowry I have been discussing fits well within this framework. If this kind of transfer were to be abolished, it would have to be in the context of a major political change where private property itself came under attack. Such a change is probably more unlikely in Australia than in Greece. Some observers have noted that dowry payments are on the increase in Australia among those who are now more financially secure and can afford to join the contest for prestige and privilege, as well as to share their achievement with their children. This is, after all, one of the major reasons for mi-grating – to 'give the children a better chance than they would have in Greece'. The production of a professional son or daughter (or son-in-law) is a source of pride. People congratulate the parents of a university graduate or someone who has achieved success. It is not just a case of sharing the limelight; it is considered the parents' responsibility and their achievement. Indeed, parents have often worked very hard for this success. It is certainly the dream of many migrants. And, as I have argued, the Australian economic and politico-legal system is constructed to reward and assist this kind of achievement. In moving from rural Greece to industrial Australia, Greeks have adapted institutions such as dowry to suit the different range of possibilities available in the new context. It is not, therefore, as a culturalist analysis might suggest, simply a case of importing a kind of cultural program that is reactivated by nostalgia or 'custom'.

There are other questions that arise from this examination of dowry, and it may be worth summarising a little at this point, before moving slightly further afield. We have established that presentations like these continue in Australia because:

• parents want to provide the best for their offspring;
• parental generosity reflects honour on the family;
• a professional son-in-law is a prestigious acquisition;
• the new family can be more clearly established within the Australian bourgeoisie than can their parents; and
• Australian economic structures were developed to protect and assist those who have accumulated capital and want to 'keep it in the family'.

They may also continue because of a relative shortage of 'suitable' sons-in-law in Australia. I have outlined some of the demographic and cultural factors that have created such a shortage in Greece, such as increasing urbanisation, rural stagnation and changing sexual mores. Other relevant factors include unemployment and under-employment. It is very difficult to find a secure job in Athens or Thessaloniki. A man with such a job, especially a white collar job, is certain to be over-valued in the marriage market. If one takes into account male unwillingness to marry and the increasing sexual freedom I mentioned earlier, the market situation becomes even more stringent. In addition, virginity may still be an important consideration. According to Peristiany, one of the reasons why families make such efforts to provide dowries is that they are concerned that their daughters will lose their honour if they remain unmarried for long. It is not surprising that dowry payments have increased as parents try to 'enhance the attractiveness' of their daughters in a competitive market (see Peristiany, 1976, p.17).

Greek-Australian women may face a similar scarcity of suitable husbands. Second-generation men are increasingly marrying women of non-Greek background, and the potential source of Greek immigrant men has dried up as the migration flow has reversed. Some second-generation women go to Greece and bring back husbands, whose fares and establishment in Australia then represent a kind of dowry payment. But the differential treatment of young men and women does mean that more men than women have the opportunity to meet non-Greeks. Women, therefore, are not marrying out at the same rate, and may not marry at all. Certainly, eligible men are surrounded by prospective brides and their families. At the same time, evidence suggests that Greek-Australian girls are very marriage-oriented, despite their relatively high standard of education and career training (see Bottomley, 1980; Strintzos, 1984). Some parents feel threatened by the thought of allowing their daughters out into the non-Greek world. And this world is undoubtedly more permissive, in general, less concerned with virginity and closely-guarded sexual morality. As a result, Greek women can be trapped between the traditional morality of their parents and a decreasing opportunity to meet and marry a 'suitable' husband. They must also face a highly competitive marriage market.

Goody and Tambiah see dowry ('diverging devolution' in their terminology) as an indication of male control (1973, p.25). Although it provides women with property, it is property which devolves on marriage, thus emphasising the search for a husband. An unmarried woman can make a claim on her inheritance, but traditionally the dowry payment is negotiated and elevated in a competition over marriage. Furthermore, it is usually domestic property, which, as Allen has pointed out, redefines the domestic sphere as female (Allen, 1979). While it may indeed provide a bride with more power than she would otherwise have, it is still power within the domestic sphere.

In a small study I made of male–female relations in Greek households in Sydney, I discovered that the women with real power over decision-making were those who shared business interests with their husbands, actually participating in the production of the main source of household income (Bottomley, 1974). This kind of economic power compares with the ownership of productive agricultural land under traditional dowry arrangements. Correspondingly, the drive to acquire a professional or clerical worker as a husband suggests that a good job is itself a desirable form of property. Indeed the law increasingly regards employment as property. Both employment potential and superannuation payments are taken into account in property settlements at divorce.

In theory, then, the effort to acquire a good son-in-law could be replaced by an equivalent effort on behalf of the women themselves. This is, of course, to reverse patriarchal ideology, but the ideology is in question both in Australia and in Greece. Lambiri-Dimaki suggests that increasing education and economic progress will eventually lead to the demise of the dowry (1972). In fact, many Greek-Australian women are well-educated. Some have told me that their professional educations are regarded as a form of dowry, because they have income-earning potential. But it is still predominantly men who are trained for high status and high income-earning professions.

CONCLUSIONS

This chapter has traced the negotiation of economic, symbolic and cultural capital in the transformation of practices that are usually glossed as 'traditions'. As a set of practices with a very long history in Greece, dowry has become interwoven with some of the most basic ideas about honour, morality, self-respect and relations between men and women. At the same time, it is an economic transaction that has implications for structures of class and status, as I have demonstrated here.

The move to abolish dowry in Greece has been supported by those who criticise the increasing pressure on families, the definition of women as commodities and the taxation avoidance inherent in the current practice of dowry. Many, probably most, Greek-Australians would voice the same criticisms. Those who are socialists also criticise the maintenance of class-based privileges. But the practice remains among some segments of the Greek population because it is an approved way of establishing daughters, it consolidates a class position and reflects a limited marriage market. It also helps to bind children more closely to their family of origin and to define the expected range of choice for girls.

From this brief consideration of dowry, it appears that legal abolition will have to be accompanied by much wider changes in property and taxation laws, for example, as well as in patriarchal ideology. It also appears that the law only limits the possibilities of action, rather than defining practices *per se*. In Greece, patriarchal authority still ensures male control of property, despite the safeguards built in to the Civil Code for dower property. In Australia, taxation and property law ensure a continuation of class-based inequalities on the marriage market, as on other markets. The less formal structures of Greek kinship and social networks encourage the continuation of familism, and a form of dowry as part of the competition for symbolic as well as for economic capital.

Much of the opposition to dowry in Greece came from feminists and others who supported the argument that the practice 'commodified' women and represented marriage as a burden for which men should be compensated. But a concentration on gender equality alone obscured the economic aspect, the strategies for consolidating family capital and establishing the next generation. Although these are usually male strategies, formulated and carried out by men, they can also provide women with a valuable material base. Obviously, the negative consequences of dowry fall most heavily on women from poor families.

Some of this interweaving of class, gender and power will be discussed in the following chapter, in an exploration of the cultural construction of gender relations in Greece.

PART III

Constructing identities: gender, class and ethnos

CHAPTER 7

The cultural construction of gender in modern Greece

When we examine aspects of experience as intimate as those
of gender and sexuality, the concept of hegemony helps alert
us to the fact that the dynamics of power in the social
relations of individuals who are acting and interacting as
sexual beings can be extremely subtle and complex.

Cowan, 1990, p.14

This chapter will take up several of the themes delineated in earlier chapters. One of these is the continuing project of interrelating social, economic and political circumstances and cultural practices. A second is the process of social power, especially the definition of what is 'imaginable'. A third is the development of some understanding of the cultural construction of gender in both meanings and values and in practices through which these values are expressed and embodied. Several other themes are also woven into this analysis – for example, the interplay between the subjective and objective and the possibly distorting effects of particular perspectives and analytic frameworks. To this end, I propose to observe the observers, to ask how gender relations have been represented in recent studies of modern Greece. As Paul Rabinow put it, representations are also social facts and deserve scrutiny (1986). Feminist writers have made major contributions to questioning of this kind, from Juliet Mitchell's *Woman's Estate* (1971) to the complex critiques of phallocentric discourses that have attacked the linguistic and philosophical foundations of self-evident authority (see Pateman and Gross, 1986).

Other writers, such as Said (1985), have demonstrated the ethnocentrism and political bias of Orientalist scholars, and anthropologists are increasingly aware of a crisis in representation (cf. Clifford and Marcus, 1986). With reference to Calvino, I suggested in chapter 1 that sociology must also try to 'know itself and distrust itself'. The task is a mammoth one, since both writers and readers approach

105

their subjects with what Bourdieu describes as 'les lunettes de leur habitus' ('the spectacles of their habitus') (1980, p.41). Some biases and absences, then, will be more apparent than others, and more or less apparent to some rather than to others.

Looked at within the framework of the politics of culture, studies of modern Greece show how the adoption of particular paradigms has indeed created absences and, to some extent, misrepresentations. It is not a question of accusation or guilt, but of moving some way towards a more reflexive account which could reveal the possible influences of those 'spectacles of habitus'.

In their discussion on 'contextualising feminism', Anthias and Yuval-Davis (1983) attempted the difficult task of interrelating the three perspectives of class, ethnicity and gender, pointing out that concentration on one or another of these leads to neglect of the others. We have seen some of the consequences of this kind of separation in discussions about ethnicity, and I will refer more closely to the argument of Anthias and Yuval-Davis in the next two chapters, which deal more specifically with ethnicity, gender and class. For the present, I want to take up their point about the *intersection* of these three divisions and the separations imposed by particular paradigms. I will broaden the scope a little to include other perspectives, such as urbanism, that intrude into these studies and cannot be encompassed within the three divisions they mention.

Rabinow has proposed

an oppositional position, one suspicious of sovereign powers, universal truths, overly relativised preciousness, local authenticity, moralisms high and low. Understanding is its second value, but an understanding suspicious of its own imperial tendencies. It attempts to be highly attentive to (and respectful of) difference, but is also wary of the tendency to essentialize difference. (1986, p.258)

This seems to me an admirable starting point, but it raises problems explicitly recognised by theorists of difference, who point out that, even in opposition, we are spoken to by the very categories we hope to oppose. Thus, in the discussion that follows, I am aware that I (and other writers) use dichotomies to criticise dichotomous schemata. Reviewing the intersection of feminism and social science, Michelle Rosaldo posed the dilemma:

... at the same time that our scholarly writings have revealed the limitations of a set of categories that political concerns have taught us to distrust, they have not yet created discourses that show consistently how we can begin to do without those categories or even radically to revise them. As critics, we feminists have remained, not surprisingly, the partial victims of the categories provided by our society. (1983, p.93)

STUDIES OF MALE–FEMALE RELATIONS IN GREECE

Despite a relative neglect of modern Greece (see Herzfeld 1987), many writers have been fascinated by gender in ancient Greece. Robert Graves's *The White Goddess* (1961), and the earlier studies of scholars such as Bachofen, Frazer and Engels have generated rich and absorbing discussions about matriarchy. More recently, feminist writers have revived the idea of an ancient matriarchy to support arguments that women were not always 'the second sex' (cf. de Beauvoir, 1949; Davis, 1972). An excellent evaluation of these theories is provided by Monique Saliou (1986) in a detailed account of the processes of women's subordination in primitive and archaic Greece. Although I have no wish to enter the debate about matriarchy, I believe that some of Saliou's conclusions are also pertinent to an analysis of representations of gender in modern Greece. Their pertinence has nothing to do with purported continuities in Greek history, but with the problem of perspectives and the understanding of gender.

For example, Saliou points out that Bachofen and other nineteenth-century scholars could not accept the idea that matrilineal descent and a feminised religion could co-exist with a masculine power structure. In fact, an examination of the archaeological, literary and mythical evidence reveals webs of contradictions and complexity that are greatly over-simplified in most accounts. Greek tragedy and comedy also dramatised real conflict between the sexes, as well as an element of feminine ridicule of masculine values. From the sixth century on, philosophers increasingly sought to construct a rational system of thought based on the opposition of contraries. In Saliou's words:

Dualist classifications, inevitably symbolized by male and female, gradually gained the upper hand. Woman became, in essence, all that is most alien to man. The elements of the cosmos were themselves organized in hierarchical order. (1986, p.204)

These dualist oppositions have continued to dominate Western thought to such an extent that their self-evident nature disguises their political dimensions (cf. Lloyd, 1984). As we will see, dichotomous systems apparently abound in modern Greece. But, on closer investigation, complexities, contradictions and absences emerge that suggest other ways of perceiving gender relations.

In 1986, Michael Herzfeld diagnosed the analysis of rural Greek gender ideology as suffering from 'an excess of generalization' (p.215). Herzfeld believes that the meticulous particularism of earlier ethnographic accounts – especially those of Friedl (1962) and Campbell (1964), which have been highly influential – separated women and men from each other 'with a rigidity that far surpassed that of the actors they sought to describe', thus ignoring the 'lability of male and female stereotypes and their capacity for variation and change' (ibid.). One of the problems, as he sees it, is the concentration on a local frame of reference, to the neglect of questions of national identity. Non-Greek anthropologists tend to distinguish their own 'objective' studies from the polemics of Greek folklorists, who are thus viewed as ideologues. But Herzfeld suggests that the intense focus on gender roles is itself a distortion:

In particular, the tendency to treat the private–public phenomenon as an epiphenomenon of the female–male polarity says something about the concerns of anthropologists, but not necessarily about those of the people they study. (1986, pp.216–17)

He goes on to claim, instead, that the immense evocative power of gender categories makes them 'an ideal device for negotiating the complex relationships between different levels of identity – kin group, local, regional and national' (p.217). The apparent contradictions within gender categories reflect the complexities of these relationships.

Herzfeld then explores the category of the 'female' in Greek national identity, arguing that Greeks use a Hellenist and a Romeic model of this national culture. The first represents the archaising, European-oriented tendency that I mentioned in chapter 5. The Romeic is less classical, more domestic and incorporates some of the Byzantine and Turkish elements of Greek history. In general, women are more closely identified with the Romeic model, men with the Hellenic. However, Herzfeld concludes that, like all symbols, the markers male and female, Hellene and Romios, are extremely labile. Studying 'gender roles' in isolation from the symbolism of gender or the political rhetoric of identity means that we risk 'a reductionist binarism that separates categories from experience and represents men and women in Greek society at large as the slaves of stereotypes that are at times demonstrably inaccurate' (pp.232–3). Herzfeld, then, argues against a perceived ethnocentric and androcentric bias in representations of gender relations in Greece and directs attention to other levels of analysis. One such level that is particularly significant in Greece is kinship, another is religion.

Ernestine Friedl's now classic study of the village of Vasilika (1962) stresses the centrality of kinship in social relations. Three of the six chapters in her book are headed 'The Family and . . .'. In these three chapters, she discusses consumption habits, dowry and inheritance and economic activities – reversing the order by which the family is usually subsumed under categories such as the economy, alliance strategies and so on. In a later study, she again shows the importance of kinship in facilitating rural–urban migration, and in linking the village with the city (1976). Her recognition of the centrality of the family and of the power of women within the family leads Friedl to argue for a re-assessment of the role of rural women (1967). Nevertheless, she emphasises the fundamental opposition of male and female, in relations marked by complementarity rather than struggle.

This notion of a complementary opposition also appears in du Boulay's study of a village in Euboea where men have, in her words, 'a relative divinity', but women are 'from the Devil', the weak link through which man can become vulnerable to evil. Men are described as clean and pure (*katharoi*) whereas women are polluting (*vroma*). Du Boulay stresses, however, that women also have a potential divinity which provides them with the means of fulfilling their highest role, that of wife and mother. In marriage, therefore, there is a symbiosis, a partnership between equals (1974).

In a later paper, du Boulay argues that the apparent contradictions in the representations of women as 'equal to the Mother of God', on the one hand, and 'Eve, the destroyer of houses', on the other, do not constitute two different world views or an appearance and reality that are logically opposed.

Rather, it is suggested that they are two different aspects of a concept of feminine nature that is rooted ultimately in a religious vision of humanity, a vision that sees the role of women in terms of two allied but ultimately very different ideas – those of feminine nature and feminine potentiality. (1986, pp.144–5)

In the same volume, Herzfeld goes further, to suggest that

It is . . . not so much that women are flawed in Greek gender ideology, as that they can stand for the flaws, as well as the benefits, that Greeks recognise as characteristic of their own families, villages, regions, and even nation. Herein lies the significance of women as simultaneously virginal mothers, and diabolical strumpets. (1986, p.217)

Herzfeld's own account of the association of women with what I have called 'muted cultural modes' is reinforced in a beautiful paper by Anna Caraveli on the lament as social protest (1986). Caraveli describes these practices as 'a universe of female activity outside the realm of men' (p.169). In Caraveli's words,

Although based on the village's larger system of values and interpretations, this universe had its own variants of these, while many of the tasks, social roles and expressive genres were gender specific, limited to women only. (pp.169–70)

Moreover, men and urbanised women expressed disapproval of the laments, which also earned the official displeasure of the Church. In fact, some of the laments she recorded present non-Christian attitudes, such as despair, fear and anger towards death and the deceased, rather than patience and acceptance. They also refer to Hades and Charon, rejecting the Christian notion of a rewarding after-life for the pious. However, the artistic qualities of these laments were admired by men, especially by folk musicians, and men knew of the compositions and performance of laments. Men also sing publicly about death, as in the magnificent and well-known *moiroloyia* from Epiros. Laments are part of a wider poetic tradition of commentary on political events and individual crises, such as emigration, marriage and widowhood, as well as the fall of cities and the deaths of heroes. In the case of the women's laments, Caraveli argues that we can gain insight into the lament's use by and for the living and its fluid, continuously adaptive nature by focussing on their mediation at the points of overlap between such seemingly disparate and antithetical categories as 'male–female; traditional–modern; sacred–secular and ideological–actual, as well as between formal institutions and the individual or domestic needs not accommodated by them' (1986, p.178). Caraveli sees these laments as articulating the tragedy of everyday life. The women who perform them are 'creators of coping strategies, artists, critics, articulators, and manipulators of one of Greece's most important verbal arts in continuous existence' (p.192).

Caraveli's paper reveals the practices of women within a kind of poetics of identity. As I argued in chapter 4, there is a relative neglect of such expressions of feeling in ethnographies and in sociology. Greeks themselves actually talk about them a good deal – for example, about *kefi*, which Caraveli describes as a heightened emotional state. It is frequently seen as the point of socialising, especially of dancing and singing. Jane Cowan's study of dance events (1990), discussed in chapter 5 above, analyses the importance of *kefi*, noting that *kefi* can mark the heights of sociability as well as its potential disruption. It is also said that a house without a woman lacks *kefi*. Perhaps these expressions are part of the concealed mode Herzfeld refers to, or perhaps the ethnocentrism of our conceptual frameworks dictates the priorities of what we observe.

The dualisms of earlier studies has been challenged in more recent work, some of which has been written from a feminist perspective. Renée Hirschon, for example, demonstrates that the distinction between sacred and secular (and /or sacred and profane) is not so clear-cut in Greece where, for hundreds of years, to be Greek meant to be Christian and where all rites of passage were, until recently, religious rituals (1983). There is a constant interpenetration of the sacred and the secular in rituals of commensality, the pervasiveness of household icons, and the celebrations of religious festivals (*paniyiria*). Hirschon also challenges the public–private distinction, arguing that women are responsible for the spiritual life of the family, which extends beyond the domestic, especially in the commemoration of the dead and in visits to shrines on behalf of the family. Hirschon warns that we may too easily impose a Western model of religion on Greece, as though our assumptions were not problematic.

This view is supported by Dubisch's study of women's religious activities. According to Dubisch, if we view Greek women's relationship to the sacred only in terms of the negative symbolism assigned to femaleness, we may overlook the fact that women are responsible for the spiritual wellbeing of the family 'not just by controlling their pollution and sexuality, but also through the positive actions of healing and nurturing' (1983, p.194).

Moreover, a closer examination of the notion of pollution reveals that it refers not only to femaleness, but to the broader area of bodily functions and the control which should be exercised over them. Men's bodily excretions are also polluting and potentially dangerous, and even male sexuality must be controlled and disciplined. The term *varvatos* – well endowed with testicles and the strength purported to come from them – may also describe the dishonourable conduct of a rapist or bully. Dubisch argues that women, by controlling the chaotic forces of nature, operate more in the realm

of culture than of nature. But her main thesis is that such dichotomous schemata misrepresent the complexities of gender symbolism
and social interaction.

Dubisch and another anthropologist, Ruth Mandel (1983) see
women as important mediators, controlling and creating boundaries
but also acting as bridges between the areas thus delineated. Women
are usually incorporated into the households of their husbands,
thereby representing both 'ours' and 'theirs' in the opposition between
families. They are also liminal to both life and death, bearing and
delivering babies and caring for the dead and the dying. And their
religious practices may include some not necessarily acceptable
to the Church, although, as we have seen, they are the spiritual
guardians of the family.

The theme of ambivalence is also emphasised by Muriel Dimen,
who, locating her studies within a broader political context, shows
the structural contradictions that have to be negotiated by women,
especially as villagers become more dependent on the state and
modernisation increases. Her very subtle analysis reveals domestic
relations as recreating not only wider social structures, but also their
contradictions:

and so what child and adult absorb from the domestic process of social
reproduction is both social compliance and social criticism. (1983, p.233)

For example, the women in her fieldwork village in Epiros worked
alone, doing all the household tasks, including the gathering of
brushwood for ovens. Their isolation made them feel lonely, but
they wore their loneliness with pride, communicating to their
children and kin the necessity of autonomy, but also helping to create
people potentially isolated from each other. Similarly, the women
carried heavy burdens and praised their own strength, worked
unceasingly and boasted of their fatigue. They swept the floors with
three-foot brooms, saying that only old weak women need long
handled brooms (p.236). As Dimen describes it,

Their stout-hearted exhaustion communicates to the young how to suffer
well and how, also, to struggle well; how to handle the need to work hard
in a hard world and how to resist the personal erosion brought about by
grappling with it. Their merry resistance helps the young become hard
workers for themselves and their families. (p.237)

The message comes across that drudgery is systemic and widespread,
but perhaps overdetermined. And the efforts that women expend

within the household serve to soften but also to reveal the relative lack of power of their men, who, as peasants or part-time proletarians, are hardly the all-powerful males of the symbolic dichotomy.

All these writers challenge dichotomous schemata and emphasise process, negotiation and contradictions. Jane Cowan's study (1990) is explicitly concerned with contestations and pluralities. Cowan argues that the kind of gender complementarity described by Friedl and du Boulay 'must always be seen in the context of a broader asymmetry of male dominance of the androcentric and patriarchal institutions through which it is manifested' (p.11). Cowan tries to avoid dichotomies such as traditional–modern and rural–urban, but recognises ways in which such dichotomies were appropriated 'for use as symbolic terms within local discourses, both verbal and non verbal' (p.231) and in the negotiation of identities, positions and power relations. Understood in this different sense, dichotomies are obviously important elements of the politics of culture.

FAMILY, POLITICS AND ECONOMY

By questioning dichotomous models and scrutinising theoretical frameworks, the writers I have been discussing are able to locate male–female representations within the wider context of social relations – offering, I believe, a much more dynamic view of Greek culture and society and challenging some of the 'eternal verities' of that other eternal verity, 'traditional culture'. They have also taken up the motif of the family, which, as I argued earlier, is not usually analysed in relation to wider economic, political and ideological contexts. Muriel Dimen has suggested one such analysis, Juliet du Boulay and Renée Hirschon have demonstrated the universalising aspects of women's spiritual responsibilities. Ruth Mandel and Jill Dubisch emphasise the fact that women mediate between those most basic of political units, competing family groups.

It is my contention that our understanding of the genuine centrality of the Greek family may have been blurred by Western models of the nuclear family. There is a strong element of Parsonianism in the public–private dichotomy (cf. universalistic men–particularistic women; instrumental men–expressive women, etc.), which I will analyse further in chapter 9. We have already seen some of the problems of such dichotomies, and we should be particularly wary of applying them to a country like Greece, where the family is a kind of corporate enterprise for which everyone, even a small child, bears some responsibility.

In the economic sphere, for example, the capitalist mode has not displaced the family-based unit of simple commodity production. Jennifer Cavounidis has pointed out some of the consequences of this fact in relation to women's work in Greece. To quote Cavounidis,

> The family is the main economic cell of Greek society, and it is the family that decides which members will carry out which economic activities. It is also the unit of status and, because honour is at stake, the family has to weigh the social costs against economic benefits derived from the economic activity of its women. (1983, p.323)

It is worth pointing out that most Greek women are, and have been, economically active – not only as houseworkers, but as domestic producers – and that a high proportion of Greek industry is still family-based. But 87 per cent of women agriculturalists enumerated in the 1971 census, for example, were described as 'family aides', and women do not have a recognised right to allocate family income – even if that income was derived from their own dowries. Moreover, women in paid work tend to be wage earners (75.8 per cent of women workers cf. with 53.4 per cent of male workers were in this category in 1971), whereas men are more likely to be self employed (27.8 per cent cf. with 4 per cent of women workers) (Cavounidis, 1983, p.331, table III). And most women wage workers do not earn enough to make an independent living; in 1975, the average female wage was only 68 per cent of the average male wage in Greece (Psacharapoulos, 1983, p.342, table IV). Again, ideas about masculinity and femininity suggest that women are materially dependent on men and that control over their labour is predicated on their lack of access to an independent living (Cavounidis, p.338).

There is some variation to this pattern, however, that indicates the need for a more complex analysis than a concentration on gender will allow. A relatively high proportion of Greek women workers are professionals (7 per cent of women cf. with 5.1 per cent of men) (Psacharapoulos, p.353). An increasing number of women are now also working in the public service (Tsoucalas, 1986). The crucial point here, of course, is about access to educational qualifications. Although there is considerable educational mobility in Greece, women are still over-represented at the other end of the spectrum. A recent study revealed that 78 per cent of illiterates in Greece were women (Topping, 1983, p.7). It is also true that Greek women are found at the top of the administrative hierarchy, as parliamentarians. But a study of the 13 women members of the Assembly in 1981 showed that all these women came from families of political note 'with a more or less stable clientele' (Dritsas, 1981, p.5). For example, the famous Melina Mercouri, recently Minister for Culture, is the daughter of a former Mayor of Athens.

I am not suggesting that women politicians could not succeed without such a family background. What I am saying is that families and politics are very closely interrelated in Greece – and may be more in our own societies than models that stress universalism and meritocracy suggest. In Greece, it is far from insignificant that Andreas Papandreou is the son of a great former Prime Minister, nor is the family heritage insignificant to Andreas's son George, also a prominent politician. For women, family status can obviously cut across the limitations of femaleness. Women at this level are firmly located in the public domain.

A closer investigation of the centrality of the family in the political sphere could, I believe, reveal both androcentric and Eurocentric assumptions. As Papandreou and others reiterate, Greece is a Mediterranean and a Balkan country, with very close ties to the Middle East and to North Africa. It cannot be pressed too rigorously into Western models of understanding.

This leads me back to the problem of perspectives. Students of Greece can too easily assume, as Muriel Dimen once stated, that our studies mean 'coming to terms with our own world' (1976, p.3). No doubt the studies reflect on our own world, but we need to be aware of differences, while trying to avoid a kind of Orientalism. I have tried to demonstrate some of the possible sources of bias in studies of modern Greece, particularly in the representation of male–female relations. I have omitted a great deal, including the effects of the kind of rapid and pervasive social change suggested in Muriel Dimen's 1983 paper. Some of these effects are described by Mariella Doumanis in a study of mothering in Greece (1983). Doumanis, a practising psychologist, compares the relatively supportive networks of rural villages with the isolation and anomie of Athens, where young mothers in their small apartments struggle to follow the advice of experts in magazines and television shows. Doumanis perhaps overdraws the rural–urban contrast and relies heavily on such unquestioned dichotomies as traditional–modern. But the point remains that migration, mass media and 'modernisation' have created an entirely different social environment for city dwellers and, increasingly, for rural people.

THE CHALLENGE OF FEMINISM

Another relatively recent development that challenges the objectivity of observers is the Greek women's movement. Feminism as a political movement has been somewhat neglected in non-Greek studies of gender relations in Greece, though Cowan's book is a notable exception. One of the editors of an excellent collection of papers on women and men in Greece (the first issue of the *Journal of Modern Greek Studies*, May, 1983) told me that they had intended to include some feminist papers, but that no suitable papers were available at that stage (Allen, pers. comm.). It may also be true that the emphasis on rural women in most of these studies directed attention away from the largely city-based feminist activities. But, as we have seen, the rural–urban separation is somewhat artificial and middle-class urban women do not have a monopoly on feminism in Greece.

Eleni Stamiris, founding director of the Mediterranean Women's Studies Centre in Athens, has written an informative account of the Greek women's movement (1986) which begins with the 'first wave' of feminism in the mid-nineteenth century, mostly among middle-class women who were influenced by ideas from western Europe. The first woman student was admitted to the University of Athens in 1890. But economic and political crises pushed the 'woman question' into the background and most women were 'left behind as unpaid custodians of a subsistence agricultural system' (p.101). Middle-class women's demands for rights were stifled by the dictatorship of Metaxas after 1936, and the ensuing war, occupation and Civil War. The efforts of women were crucial during this period, however, not only as supporters but as partisan fighters. During the German occupation, men and women were deemed equal citizens in the liberated zones.

Part of the heritage of the Metaxas regime, however, was the *Civil Code*, formulated in 1940 and deriving in part from the family policies of the Nazis, which were admired by Metaxas. Under this code the male household head had absolute authority over his wife and children (*patria potestas*), and women were legal minors. Not surprisingly, Greek women could not vote or become candidates for election until 1954. And, as I suggested earlier, their employment experiences have been linked to this minority status. They are still marginalised workers, largely excluded from the paid workforce, providing unpaid labour on farms and in small businesses. Where they do paid work, it is often in the informal economy, as outworkers or domestic labourers. Until 1982, married women could not even legally establish a business without their husbands' consent. They were perceived as dependents and, as we saw in chapter 6, they required dowries to relieve the burden of this dependence. Greek women did not, therefore, share the employment experience of women in more industrialised countries during the 1950s and 1960s, except as immigrants facing the constraints and additional hardships of such a status.

Since the overthrow of the junta in 1974, there have been a number of formal changes in male–female relations. The first mass-based women's organisations were associated with parties on the Left. There have been tensions between women's objectives and party programs and feminism is sometimes seen as 'an import of decadent cultural imperialism'. But the women's organisations have large memberships (the Union of Women of Greece claimed 15,000 members in 1986, according to Stamiris).

And women are increasingly important as voters. From 1981, the PASOK government enacted major policy changes, with the new Family Law I discussed in chapter 6, the extension of pensions and medical cover, the establishment of child care centres and parental leave for both parents, maternity allowances, community health centres and the encouragement of women to join agricultural co-operatives as full members (an option not previously open to women). More recently, women have campaigned for free and legal abortion, for sex education and contraceptive advice in schools and for family planning centres, as well as for equality in the workplace. The former issues probably challenge the androcentrism of party leaders more thoroughly than the latter, but abortion, for example, is an important public health issue in a country where an estimated 250–300,000 illegal abortions are performed annually (Stamiris, 1986) in a population of some four million women of child-bearing age.

Although Greek women are still politically and economically marginalised, feminism, broadly defined, is by no means marginal. The political history of modern Greece has included women as combatants and even heroines. The huge demonstrations for peace and against pollution mobilise thousands of women, and women are continually offering an alternative, humanist, vision of a world where people matter more than power or property. To some extent, these concerns reflect more traditional preoccupations with family and children, but they are projected as universal themes that have great evocative power among people who value the familiar.

Obviously, an understanding of the relation of rural women to the wider women's movement would require very detailed and specific analyses. Once again, Jane Cowan's work is illuminating in its sensitive interweaving of political and personal concerns of the women in her fieldwork town of Sohos, and especially the influence of feminist ideas on younger women (Cowan, 1990). A number of Greek researchers are also working on projects involving village women, and the results of their work will be extremely interesting. For my purposes here, it will be enough to return to my earlier quotation from Calvino and urge scepticism about frameworks of understanding. For example, Susan Buck Sutton describes the somewhat paradoxical process whereby urban migrants from the island of Amorgos become more rather than less domesticated as a result of the move; they are also expected to provide higher and higher dowries (1986). This is part of the process of economic marginalisation discussed earlier, but it runs counter to easy assumptions about urbanism leading to a kind of liberation. At the same time, I have tried to show that feminism should not be too readily dismissed as an imposition of Western ideas. The terrains of struggle, the particular concerns of feminists and their political practices are distinctive and mark an important dimension of modern Greek life.

Certainly, Greek scholars who write about male–female relations have explicitly political concerns (cf. Kaklamanakis, 1972; Nikolaidou, 1979). But even where relations of power are more implicit, there are recurring themes that suggest some of the reasons why Greek women are not merely the patient victims of oppression. I have argued that one of these themes is the centrality of the family at all levels of Greek life. Another, I believe, is the influence of women as spiritual guardians of their families. This duty certainly entails the support of a patriarchal Church, but, as we have seen, women's religious activities are not always approved by the Church. And spiritual concerns need not be confined to formally defined religious activities. Dubisch and others have shown the symbolic significance of the house, which is the special responsibility of women (Dubisch,

1986). Moreover, as I have tried to demonstrate, this responsibility is not limited to a 'private' sphere. The household (*nikokyrio*) is, to quote two observers, 'a fundamental organizational construct in both public and private economic sectors' (Salamone and Stanton, 1986, p.98). Following Bourdieu, one can go even further and argue that symbolic capital

which in the form of the prestige and renown attached to a family and a name is readily convertible back into economic capital, is perhaps *the most valuable form of accumulation* in a society in which the severity of the climate . . . and the limited technical resources . . . demand collective labour. (1977, p.179)

According to Bourdieu, the 'ethnocentric naiveties of economism' (p.177) have set up symbolic interests in opposition to strictly economic interests, separated from 'spiritual' and 'cultural' activities.

Another important but subdued theme is the one I have called a 'poetics of identity'. Herzfeld tells us that 'the Greek woman functions, literally and metaphorically, as an apt trope for the condition of the Greek generally' (1986, p.232). This implies that the very notion of 'Greekness' is intricately associated with the cultural creation of gender, even where, as in Hellenism, women are apparently secondary. As Herzfeld sees it, the *disemia* (dual symbolism) of Greekness also includes the more domestic, more feminine model of 'Romios'. But, according to Herzfeld, women also symbolise self-knowledge. 'Their very existence is an appropriate metaphor for that condition' (p.217). What emerges from the studies discussed in this chapter is that, although women are undoubtedly constrained and marginalised by male-dominated structures, they are also creators and guardians of a symbolic universe that has its influences on a wider society. To some extent, the formal separation of women from activities defined as male has enabled them to develop such a universe, while remaining firmly within the mainstream of Greek culture.

This is by no means to deny the existence of modes of domination or the economic and political marginalisation of Greek women, which I have described above. Nor am I attempting to glorify something like a culture of the oppressed. I am arguing that closer attention to muted modes and to the limits of analytic frameworks suggests a complexity and richness that is lost in highly structured accounts. It also suggests that the 'divided world' of much Greek ethnography is itself a complex representation that obscures interrelations and ambiguities, and excludes important political dimensions, partly generated by the very imposition of categories. From a feminist perspective, therefore, it is particularly important to question the zones of silence inhabited by women, as well as to question the extent to which we – as participants and observers – re-draw the limits of those zones.

In the two concluding chapters, we will see that some of these zones of silence can be compounded in migration studies by unexamined assumptions about the supposed docility and backwardness of immigrant women, as well as by the additional silences imposed by linguistic and cultural differences and the purported 'inferiority' of immigrants. Detailed analyses like the one presented in this chapter can help to break down categorising of this kind, as well as to establish an awareness of (a) the links between cultural constructs of gender and those of 'ethnos', kinship, religion and morality; and (b) the ways in which particular analytic frameworks can lead to exclusions and misrepresentations.

CHAPTER 8

Generating identities:
age, social bodies and habitus

Identity is formed at the unstable point where the
'unspeakable' stories of subjectivity meet the narratives
of history, of a culture.

Hall, 1987, p.44

Preceding chapters have traced the transformation and re-negotiation
of cultural, symbolic and economic capital in the processes of
migration and settlement. Particular cultural practices are emphasised to maintain a sense of ethnic honour or to consolidate
cultural and economic capital – similar strategies are employed by
the autochthonous members of immigrant-receiving societies.
Indeed, they are an integral part of what I have called 'the politics
of culture' in all societies. But they are not always conscious
strategies; they often arise from beliefs that have dropped below the
level of consciousness and become taken-for-granted, apparently
'natural'. (It is not irrelevant that migrants are 'naturalised' rather
than 'nationalised'.) Moreover, those beliefs and practices that have
the status of boundary markers (especially language and religion,
but also other attributes of ethnic honour) can have immense
emotional and motivational power, as well as the capacity to
mobilise resistance against discrimination, racism and more subtle
forms of negative identification. We have also seen instances of both
positive and negative aspects of shared ethnicities.

Analyses based on static notions about the maintenance of
traditions or the separation of sets of relations labelled ethnic – or
gender or class or religious or linguistic – cannot convey the constant
interweaving of processes of transformation and cross-referencing in
heterogeneous societies. These processes are much more apparent
in the techniques of inter-referencing of writers and other artists who
manage to depict multifaceted experience and the reworking of
'traditional' forms within the constraints of specific social and
cultural imperatives (see chapter 4 above).

In this book I have analysed some of those processes by inter-relating material from countries of emigration and immigration, including the cultural construction of gender and class as well as ethnicity, and eschewing dichotomous models of subjective and objective understanding. I have also maintained a critical view of the frameworks of knowledge presented in the writings of social scientists (including myself) and others involved in the struggle over legitimate knowledge. At the same time, I have offered some alter-native frameworks and explored muted modes such as dance, music and literary work that suggest other ways of seeing, hearing and experiencing heterogeneity.

In this chapter, I want to pursue these themes through a discussion of the 'second generation' and of elderly migrants, especially in relation to social science constructs, but also with reference to the other themes discussed above, including a comparative viewpoint and an interweaving of objective and subjective perspectives. This chapter will also explore the concepts of habitus, identity and trajectory, mostly – but not entirely – within the context of the social fields of Greek-Australians.

HABITUS: A GENERATIVE STRUCTURALISM

In chapter 1, I suggested that Bourdieu's use of the concept of habitus offers a way through the unproductive separation of the subjective and the objective. I described habitus as 'the embodiment' of history, and I will return to that 'embodiment' later in this chapter. At present, I am interested in the link between personal trajectories and the collective memories that are implied in notions such as class, ethnicity and gender, and embedded in cultural practices. Habitus is the process whereby those who occupy similar positions in social and historical space tend to possess a certain sense of place, including categories of perception and appreciation that provide a common-sense understanding of the world, and especially of what is 'natural' or even imaginable. But these categories are themselves socially produced within very specific contexts, and they continue to mediate the experience and interpretation of changing objective conditions. Thus, the durable, transposable dispositions acquired in childhood are overlaid and transformed by adjustment to later circumstances. But those adjustments are themselves biassed by pre-existing per-ceptions, which mostly operate below the level of consciousness.

Habitus is not determining, but it is a powerful mediating construct that can predefine what is necessary or even imaginable.

Because the concept of habitus implies a dialectical relationship between structured circumstances and people's actions and perceptions, it requires a break with some of our most revered dualisms, such as determinism versus freedom, conditioning versus creativity, individual versus society, and interior versus exterior (the latter is particularly important in ideas about the body). Habitus manifests itself in practice, in action and movement, in the way one orients oneself in relation to specific social fields. For example, habitus usually forms the basis of personal relationships and what is described as 'homogamy', whereby people tend to marry partners with similar backgrounds. As Bourdieu clearly demonstrates in *Distinction* (1986), some habitus can also provide a form of cultural and symbolic capital in themselves, as is the case with the 'natural' ease and grace of those 'born to rule'.

The notion of habitus seems particularly relevant to a consideration of what has been described as 'the second generation'. In theory at least, it should be possible to see something of the reproduction and reformulation of cultural beliefs and practices as they are handed down from parents to children. It should also be possible to see some of the effects of the differing social and historical environments within which parents and children developed. Intergenerational studies can also incorporate both diachronic and synchronic perspectives, including some understanding of the experience over time of both parents and children as well as their relation to existing social structures.

The term 'second generation' is usually found in association with migration studies, to describe the offspring of immigrants – who are, of course, first generation something else, in the country of immigration. But it has also been used, notably by Raymond Williams (1978), in a broader sense. His semi-autobiographical work, *The Second Generation*, describes some of the conflicts, contradictions, adjustments and cultural ambiguities inherent in movement from rural Wales to industrial England, and from a household of industrial workers to a high status university. Images of place are very important and evocative in Williams' work, but he also conveys, especially through description of sexual encounters and political meetings, some of the emotional force of class habitus, including definitions of and challenges to what is imaginable and the sense of being an outsider, despite a degree of familiarity with the context (for example, in the experience of the central protagonist's semi-participating observation of a strike meeting organised by his father and of a cocktail party at the university where he is a postgraduate student). I mention Williams' work here because it helps to reinforce my contention that class – and gender – are also culturally constructed within specific contexts and that we need to consider the intersection of several aspects of the generation of identities. Williams' novels also tend to blur the literary and ethnographic genres in a way that enriches his theoretical propositions.

In this chapter, I will discuss some of the aspects of the reproduction of cultural beliefs and practices (including those pertaining to class and gender as well as ethnicity) throughout the lifecycle. Recognising some of the limits of my own competence, I cannot venture into areas that require psychoanalytic or psychological expertise. My discussion will be mostly sociological, although I am aware that a more detailed examination of the constitution of subjectivity would require both psychoanalytic and sociological perspectives.

Here, I begin from a position that sees cognitive structures primarily as internalised and embodied social structures. As Bourdieu has demonstrated in *Distinction* (1986), people acquire 'knowledge without concepts'. Through conditions that differentiate, through exclusions and inclusions, hierarchies and classifications inscribed in cultural practices and in institutions such as families and education systems, in the interaction of everyday life, social divisions are inscribed in people's minds. In other words, we can attribute to ourselves a 'choice' that has actually been predefined by our social conditions (as in the familiar phrase 'that's not for the likes of you and me').

LANGUAGE AND COMMUNICATION

People who share similar positions in a social field also share a set of basic schemes of perception. This does not mean a homogeneity of understanding, but certain similarities that arise from and give rise to continuing distinctions. A powerful 'objective' source of such distinctions is found in language, in pairs of opposing concepts – such as high–low; fine–coarse; brilliant–dull – that classify and qualify persons and objects. Language is obviously crucial to the process of identity formation, and habitus is strongly mediated by the assumptions implicit in language, especially the language of childhood, aptly named 'the mother tongue'. The mother tongue, of course, includes all kinds of variations, according to class, region of origin, even gender. In the case of migration, the issue of language is infinitely complicated by the magnitude of the disruption caused by movement from one major language system to another. Many of the struggles over adjustment in a new society are struggles over language, sometimes for basic understanding, sometimes for recognition.

Understandably, language has been an important mobilising force among minority groups, who have endeavoured to maintain the languages of countries of origin as well as to have access to the dominant language in countries of immigration. In the Australian case, the policy of multiculturalism has given official status to what are called 'community languages'. Some of these are taught as part of school curricula or with assistance from state authorities, for example, in Saturday classes at state schools. Nevertheless, these languages have an academic status inferior to that of the established 'foreign languages' such as French and German. This is less the case with Italian, the language of the largest non-Anglophone population in Australia and bearer of an influential high culture. Modern Greek has also been located in the Classics department of some universities and has gained a certain distinction by association with the fathers of Western civilisation.

As a long-term observer of the effects of changes in Australian policy, I have noted that one of the consequences of multiculturalism, which became operative in the mid-to-late 1970s, has been an increase in self-respect among the offspring of immigrants. When I interviewed second-generation Greek-Australians in the late 60s and early 70s, they frequently spoke about their embarrassment and isolation in relentlessly Anglophone environments, especially in schools. But the introduction of community language programmes, together with increasing numbers of students of non-English-speaking backgrounds in schools and tertiary institutions, has given non-Anglophones a much higher profile, and there has been as well important public recognition of cultural differences. Prejudice, discrimination, racism, and inequalities continue, but the field of struggle is much more open than it was during the earlier period of assimilationism.

This contrasts with France, for example, where the educational programs for immigrants are focussed on *alphabétisation* – meaning, in this case, literacy in the French language – and the battle lines are clearly drawn against pluriculturalism. The French context is different, of course, with 39 per cent of 'foreigners' being Muslim North Africans, who confront a firmly secular state system and a predominantly Catholic sub-stratum of beliefs (see Bottomley and Lechte, 1990, for some discussion of ethnic diversity and the nation-state in France). In Australia, the state education system has been 'free, compulsory and secular' since 1880, but there has always been a large Catholic school system somewhat oppositional to the (nominally) Protestant majority. Immigrants have been mainly Christian, though there is an increasing Muslim and Buddhist component. But 'private' schools (as opposed to the Catholic 'parochial' schools) have been mainly concerned with reproducing class habitus, including important forms of cultural capital generated by networks of influence. Many of the more affluent non-Anglophone immigrants – and some of the less affluent – have recognised the value of this cultural capital and sent their children to these expensive schools, where the ethnic form of the class habitus is overwhelmingly British.

George Papaellinas, whose work I introduced in chapter 4, has written a short story about a Greek-Australian boy, Peter Mavromatis, learning Ancient Greek from an elegant teacher who, with great condescension, steers his two Greek-speaking students through the dreadful shoals of their own 'corrupted' language, Modern Greek, and into the 'further dimensions' of the Ancients. In a scene that carries both the writer's compassion and the boy's confusion, he describes the elegant teacher (Roger) and a Professor of Classics faced with Peter's father enthusiastically reciting Homer. The boy discusses this scene (with himself) in the following words:

He fucks everything up, and Roger nods some more and says, 'I'm sorry, Mr. Mavromatis . . . I don't speak modern Greek,' and the idiot looks really surprised. You must have explained the difference between modern and classical pronunciation about a thousand times!

'It's the . . . how do you call it . . . the . . . you know . . . o Achilleas,' and Roger aaahs, 'The Iliad', and the old fool nods his head, would you believe he's annoyed and the professor, he just wants to piss off. He's had it, and Roger has to explain.

'We study Classical pronunciation, Mr. Mavromatis . . . I'm sorry'. (Papaellinas, 1986, pp.34–5)

Peter is also sorry, ranged with his 'betters' against his unscholarly and thus apparently unacceptable parent.

REPRESENTING THE SECOND GENERATION: FRAMEWORKS AND THEMES

Not surprisingly, language and education have been central concerns in social science studies of the second generation. Most of these studies have been policy-oriented and short term, and have tended to focus on the problems of ethnic youth (see Bottomley, 1991, for an extended discussion of some of these studies). There are certainly problems, especially those to do with language learning, unemployment, familial conflict and racism. But the more positive aspects of being someone in the middle are rarely explored. Some French writers have explicitly argued the virtues of being a *métèque* (cf. Morin, 1989; Todorov, 1989) and of recognising the stranger in ourselves (Kristeva, 1988). But we do not even have a polite term in English to describe a person of mixed origins. Interestingly, the translation of *métèque* in Le Robert and Collins' Dictionary (Français-Anglais) is 'wog' (pej.)! I will return to this point later in this chapter, when discussing representations of the second generation.

In Australia, almost half the population claims English origins, but a large proportion (67.3 per cent) is mixed – that is to say, English and something else (Price, 1987). Of that section of the population, many have the assets of bilingualism, biculturalism and a degree of adaptability not so accessible to those who have not experienced markedly different schemes of perception. Such experiences can be disorienting and even agonising, but they can also provide an understanding and tolerance of diversity as well as a potential base for challenging the taken-for-granted. I suggested these possibilities in chapters 1 and 4, and will develop them later in this chapter.

Some of the explanation for the social scientists' focus on problems lies in their aims and methods. Statistically significant snapshots provide extremely limited understandings of human lives, and the assumptions on which such studies are based are too rarely analysed. A further shortcoming (one raised in chapters 2 and 3) is of the absence or neglect of an anthropological input into migration studies. The more finely grained picture available through anthropological work is especially valuable in questioning assumed homogeneities and other forms of reductionism. Anthropologists are also increasingly aware of problems of representation; not only that of representing the other (see Fabian, 1983; Clifford and Marcus, 1986), but of recognising the other in ourselves (Herzfeld, 1987; Segalen, 1989). This increasing reflexivity has doubtless been forced upon most anthropologists by the consequences of post-colonialism, but it is much less apparent in other social sciences, despite appeals from Gouldner (1971) to Giddens (1987).

In the case of studies of migration and settlement, as I have argued earlier, social scientists, who are almost invariably concerned with social management, are also usually working within their own societies, as professionals trained within particular disciplinary frameworks. Australia's foremost sociologist of migration, the late Jean Martin – who, like Bourdieu, moved into sociology from anthropology – once referred to 'the enduring frames of reference that stand in the shadows' behind definitions of public knowledge (Martin, 1978, p.26). Her study, *The Migrant Presence*, revealed controlling tendencies in the work of even the most sympathetic of commentators. As I pointed out in earlier chapters, these tendencies can be manifested in unidimensional explanations that valorise one or another perspective and deny others; in the definition of some topics as unsuitable, marginal and trivial; in the separation of objective and subjective understandings; in the ready acceptance of binary oppositions; in the emphasis on static concepts rather than processes and practices and in the failure to scrutinise the position of the observer.

In her own work, Martin continually confronted some of these issues, offering thoughtful and detailed critiques of government policy as well as the work of social scientists and the 'helping professions' (see Martin, 1978, 1981). Her contribution, however, was by no means negative; she developed methods and explanatory models that offered ways beyond some of the problems I have out-lined above, and she maintained an awareness of her own location as a social researcher. In the late 1960s, Jean Martin undertook research on kinship forms, class and social relations in several suburbs of Adelaide, South Australia. She developed studies of social networks, especially patterns of interaction that she described as 'community type' and 'clustered'. The first showed multiple con-nections between kin and other associates (such as friends and neighbours). In the second type, clusters of interaction were more clearly separated (Martin 1967, 1970). To a considerable extent, this mode of analysis located her research subjects within specific social fields and provided an idea of process and social practices that complemented her information about the people's perceptions of their lives.

Jean Martin's work has influenced my own research in a number of ways. For our purposes in this chapter, it is worth retracing some of the aspects of that research that have been particularly concerned with second-generation Greek-Australians. The book based on my doctoral research, *After the Odyssey*, was also mentioned in chapter 3, in the discussion about abstractions such as culture, class and nation in the context of migration and in relation to the individual lives of migrants and their children. My project there, as here, was to understand something of the intersection of biographies and history. *After the Odyssey* analysed the negotiation of 'Greekness' and 'Australian-ness' within specific social fields, especially those of people who could be defined by both terms – the second generation. Within a large-scale frame of the demographic, historical and cultural background of the Greek-speaking population of Sydney, I made detailed studies of 23 Greek-Australians over the age of 21 (intending to avoid the complications of adolescence, which, I believe, could account for a number of the problems that dominate the social science literature about the second generation). I interviewed these subjects at length (some 8–10 hours each, over a two-year period), joined in family and other social gatherings where possible, used a 'snowball' technique of interviewing friends and relatives to build up a composite picture of social networks. I also adapted Lewin's notion of 'life space' (1952) to represent the relative importance to each individual of various affiliations – for example, those based on kinship, work, club membership and friendship.

In the process of mapping the social worlds of my informants, I elaborated on the network analyses used in earlier studies, especially those of Martin, discussed above. These two techniques – the networks and life space diagrams – provided graphic representations of people's interactions and affiliations, that complemented their descriptions of the content of those relations.

At the same time, I outlined the parameters of what is usually called 'the Greek community', tracing the historical background to Greek-Australian settlement, the form and functions of organisations and institutions such as the Greek Orthodox Church, and the conflicts, divisions and differences that cut across this particular 'imagined community'. In anthropological terms, there are communities within the Greek-speaking population – that is, people who interact and share common values. But the entire Greek-Australian population is not a community in the sense in which anthropologists understand the word.

This early research also included, as an important part of its mapping, a model of Greek 'core culture', developed from a wide range of sources – social sciences, literature and personal statements. I have already (in chapter 3) pointed to some of the shortcomings of such a model: problems of reification, of neglecting diversity, etc. These problems are apparent in some of the more recent usages of the 'core culture' concept (see esp. Smolicz, 1981). However, my particular formulation had been constructed over many years of reading, observation and discussion with Greek-speakers and philhellenes. It takes account of historical, economic and political changes and it has been flexible enough to accommodate variations and subtleties, as indicated in chapters 5, 6 and 7 above.

This cultural model was not a kind of shopping list of 'cultural characteristics', as is too often found in books about 'understanding migrants' of one kind or another. Moreover, although it was primarily an observer's model, it included more immediate models from the experiences of specific Greek-speakers. Perhaps most important was the fact that the questions derived from this framework clearly have significance for the people with whom I have worked during some twenty years of formal research in Australia and in Greece.

After the Odyssey, therefore, bridged the objective and subjective by exploring and interrelating

• the contours of the 'Greek community' and the location of specific individuals within those contours;
• the elements of a model of Greek core culture and the cultural content of my informants' own activities; and
• the identification of my informants with these structures and practices defined as 'Greek' or 'Australian' and with other elements of their socio-cultural environments. This aspect also included identification by other people.

As I mentioned earlier, my interviewees in this study were all over the age of 21 and had been born or brought up in Australia. The study demonstrated that the majority were included in community-type social networks that 'sustained a social environment based on kinship, friendship, shared experience and mutual understanding' (Bottomley, 1979, p.129). These networks were important in maintaining and enabling commitment to Greekness, as were participation in ethnic institutions, visits to and contacts with Greece and marriage to Greek spouses. In exploring the interviewees' self-identifications and their perceptions of how they were identified by others, I found a remarkable degree of self-awareness, probably related to a sense of coping with (at least) two cultural milieux. Some of their coping strategies were developed within what I described as 'areas of conversation' with others who confirmed a particular definition of reality, and constituted a kind of moral community. In this way, negative inputs, such as prejudice and discrimination, could also be processed and resisted. Class position, status aspirations and gender were at least as important as ethnicity in the construction of these identities, but were less clearly articulated. This was partly a result of the focus of my research, but it was also the case that my second-generation informants were mostly people with professional training or the owners of small businesses. In that respect, their class position differed from that of their parents, and this very fact formed part of their *cultural* difference from their parents. The class-based element of intergenerational relations is usually missed in second-generation studies.

From this brief resumé of the research, it is clear that these second-generation subjects were both constructed by and actively constructing their social and cultural universes. In later work, I have maintained this 'subjectivist objectivism' in studies of the relevance of feminism to Greek-Australian women and girls (1983, 1984, 1984a), placing more emphasis on gender and class than was present in *After the Odyssey*. The analysis of dowry in chapter 6 above and of gender relations in Greece (chapter 7) also demonstrate that cultural practices are always contested, and that class, gender and ethnicity are always culturally and socially constructed within specific contexts.

IDENTITY AND DIFFERENCES

In a paper entitled 'Minimal Selves', Stuart Hall has commented on 'the centring of marginality', the common feeling that we have all in some way, 'recently migrated' (1987, p.44). 'Identity', Hall continued, 'is formed at the unstable point where the unspeakable stories of subjectivity meet the narratives of history, of a culture' (ibid.).

Recognising that the self is always, in a sense, a fiction, as are the various communities of identification – nation, ethnic group, families, sexualities – he suggests a 'politics of articulation'. Hall believes that 'it is an immensely important gain when we recognise that all identity is constructed across difference and begin to live with the politics of difference' (p.45).

We have seen in previous chapters that migration implies a politics of difference. Moreover, cultural practices are constructed across difference, including those of class and gender. But identity carries the implication of homogeneity. Literally, identity means 'the quality of being the same' (from the Latin, *idem*, same). The term has developed to signify identification with some imagined community, as in Hall's usage and (in, for example, the work of Erik Erikson and other psychoanalysts) a sense of consistency over time. I shall return to this usage in discussing elderly migrants later in this chapter.

In preceding chapters I have analysed the politics of culture within the negotiation of identities at some length, but I would like to make the point here that the 'second generation' is precisely defined across several imagined communities, i.e. defined in difference. This experience can be painful and hazardous, incurring alienation, racism and hostility through various forms of exclusion. The forms of identity politics embedded in cultural practices can also be regressive and limiting in certain respects. For example, restrictive definitions of gender relations may be deemed necessary to define the boundaries of ethnic groups; or ethnocentric–racist notions may be manifest in concepts of ethnic honour. The tendency to construct the world in terms of us versus them can transform imagined communities into armed camps.

Nevertheless, as Hall points out, it is important to recognise that every identity is 'placed, positioned, in a culture, a language, a history. Every statement comes from somewhere, from somebody in particular' (p.46). This does not have to mean definition by exclusion, but it can signal an important process of relativising.

This kind of relativising, of course, is strongly contested on a number of fronts. But it is literally embodied in the habitus of the second generation. As I suggested in chapter 1 and elsewhere in this book, the relativising experience of difference can also give rise to a scepticism about legitimate knowledge – or, at the very least, an ability to handle contradictory messages. It is not my intention to minimise the real pain incurred in the experience of marginality or racism. The processes of subjection are pervasive and subtle, and not easily accessible to consciousness (cf. Foucault, 1982). But the increasing recognition of counter-hegemonic challenges to principles of identity (or sameness) has opened up new terrains of struggle. Evidence suggests that this development has sharpened conflicts over what Bourdieu called 'the power to conserve or transform the objective principles of union and separation' (1987, p.163). But it has also allowed large numbers of people to understand and resist forms of domination based on those 'objective principles'.

For 'second-generation immigrants' or 'ethnics', this understanding can take a number of forms. It can lead to an ability to act as bridges between parents and the wider society, or to a deep understanding of the position of the outsider. The Italo-Australian writer, Anna Maria dell'Oso, demonstrates this kind of empathy in her essay, 'Scaling the Linguistic Wall of Indifference' (1987). Dell'Oso describes the encounter of an Asian woman with a surly bus driver whose only language is Strine (a form of Australian English, barely intelligible to many of the native-speakers). The writer, moved to rescue the woman from her tormenter, notes that translating came easily to her:

after a lifetime of crossing both sides of the language barrier, Australia's Great Wall of Indifference, which is protected by the barbed wire of custom and the watchdogs of a savage schoolyard education. (p.24)

She goes on to explain that she has been crossing this Wall since babyhood, hence,

I now have an instinct for the meaning behind broken English of nearly every culture, no matter how foreign the accent. (p.24)

Although she herself obviously communicates very well in English, her own experience as a tourist in France, trying to speak schoolgirl French to merciless Parisians reinforced her understanding of the 'fear of dumbness'. She concludes:

When I see an elderly New Australian with poor English, I remember it is often the most vulnerable who bury themselves in silence. (p.25)

In preceding chapters, I have referred to other works by second-generation writers that demonstrate a particular sensitivity to inter-subjectivities and inter-referencing. This kind of work is extremely important in relativising claims to control of legitimate knowledge or constructions of unitary 'identities'. In a way, they demonstrate some of the layers of habitus in their ability to present experience from a perspective that is not wholly their own, but has some of the immediacy of subjectivity.

As I suggested in chapter 4, this ability is especially valuable as a kind of counter-memory, a recognition that the dominant 'truths' of society obscure some experiences and emphasise others. The destruction of certain memories is a mode of subjection, and occurs in numerous ways. One is the blatant form used by various authoritarians, such as the 'airbrushing out of history' of those, like Trotsky, who became unacceptable. A more subtle form is that of simply ignoring the existence of segments of the population, in the way that women, for example, have frequently been ignored in the writing of history and other narratives.

Yet another is created by the so-called 'generation gap', whereby the younger generation is encouraged to reject the experience and understanding of their parents. This increasingly common tendency can be exaggerated in migration, where parents can also be rejected as foreign, uneducated and generally embarrassing, as we saw in the extract from George Papaellinas' story about Peter Mavromatis, his father and his Greek teacher. This kind of rejection mirrors the racism of the wider society and, of course, creates a doubly painful burden for immigrant parents. As I pointed out in *After the Odyssey*, this negative evaluation is cut across by economic 'success' in a society where individuals are blamed for 'failure'.

Under these circumstances, writers like Anna Maria dell'Oso are not only translating their own experiences with compassion and sensitivity. They are also helping to establish a 'counter-memory', narratives about the multiplicity of identities. Such narratives are increasing daily. I have mentioned a few writers, but there are also composers, musicians, painters, sculptors, potters and film-makers working on what I call 'the cultural production of diversity'. One group of writers and actors from the Federation of Italian Migrant Workers and their Families (FILEF) have produced a play and film based on the issue of intergenerational differences across three generations of women (*Tre Rosa*), with dialogue in Italian and English. FILEF's other cultural activities also emphasise bilingualism and communality rather than the separateness of Italian speakers.

Similarly, a group of Greek-Australian artists exhibited their work during the 9th Greek Festival of Sydney in 1991, under the title

'Between Cultures'. In a written introduction to this exhibition, Helen Haralambous described their project as indicating

a new consciousness, one of awareness and confidence, resulting in a shift away from struggling to avoid relegation – the threat of being overlooked as simply an ethnic artist or traditionally folkloric.

Some of the images in these paintings evoked Ancient Greece, but, in the case of one artist, Stephanie Margaritidis, these classical referents helped her to explore gender identities. Another artist, Maria Strouthos, took 'as image and symbol' the brilliantly coloured doorways that also fascinate photographers in Greece. Several paintings and sculptures were firmly located in an Australian context; one of these was John Aslanidis' silhouettes of cricketers, and Andrew Mayson's sculpture, 'The Bondi Surfer'.

A third group of young 'ethno-Australians' has been more controversial, writing and performing a provocative series of sketches called *Wogs Out of Work*. The success of their stage show was extraordinary. It ran for several years in Sydney and Melbourne and won the team a television contract for a weekly comedy entitled *Acropolis Now* – which has now, in its turn, become a stage show. Both of these productions have earned their creators strong criticism (as well as lots of money and enormous popularity). They have been accused of being co-opted, of condoning racism and sexism, of encouraging the stereotypes of migrants, etc. The writers and actors undoubtedly employ stereotypes, but these are always ironic. For example, the leading female character in *Acropolis Now*, Effie (Mary Coustas), wears clothes that she describes as 'bright, tight and tacky', and a hairstyle that maintains her long, strong hair at a considerable distance from her head by the use of 'industrial-strength hair spray'. She claims that 'her version of how the fashionable ethnic female looks is only a slight exaggeration of the real thing'. This is the process of stereotyping, but, in this case, it can also relativise and (apparently) popularise the 'real thing'. Both *Wogs Out of Work* and *Acropolis Now* contain some equally ironic parodies of Anglo-Australian racism, as well as a large dose of cheeky resistance. They have played the strategy employed by an increasing number of second-generation people, of inverting the racism and celebrating their attributed 'wogginess' in their own way. Such a celebration is inevitably double-edged, taking on a negative epithet as a symbol. But it precisely locates one of the bases for a collective counter-memory, a recognition and a surpassing of racism. As I mentioned earlier in this chapter, we have no polite word in English like the French *métèque* or the Spanish *mestizo*, but people who celebrate being in-between, while recognising the racism that partly defines such a position, have indeed begun to take up some of the space created by multiple identities.

THE SOCIO-CULTURAL CONTEXT OF AGEING

Earlier in this chapter, I pointed out the tendency of social scientists to define second generation 'ethnic Australians' as problems. This form of representation conceals many complexities, including the more positive aspects of multiple identities. Fortunately, many of those who are being represented in this way can also represent themselves. With a command of the linguistic and cultural idiom of their definers, together with an alternative understanding, they are forging their own images and 'ways of seeing'.

In this respect, the elderly are less fortunate. As their numbers increase in industrialised countries, they are increasingly defined as problems, and frequently infantilised in the process. Elderly immigrants are seen as doubly problematic, with additional complications arising from their linguistic and cultural competences. Having served their time as productive labourers, many forming the core of the industrial workforce in countries like Australia during the 1960s and 1970s, or providing the major source of population increase by reproductive labour, or both, they are now regarded as a burden, draining the resources of the state with pensions and health care provisions. Part of the irony of this position is the fact that because immigrants were selected for their suitability as workers, they were healthier than the 'host' population and, as a result, have a longer life expectancy. Except for the large number of immigrants with work-related illnesses, the immigrant population of Australia is still generally healthier than the Australian-born (McCallum, 1990).

In the case of the ageing, the social scientists are overshadowed by the medical definers, who bear the imprimatur of a properly scientific understanding. Thus, ageing is regarded as primarily a biological process, a relentless series of stages of growth. There is no question that human beings undergo processes of birth, maturation and death, or that we acquire physical and psychological competences over a period of time. But there are wide cross-cultural and historical variations in the form of those developments and in their particular saliences. Societies differ in their treatment of children and older people, according to place and time. Phillipe Ariès' fascinating study, *Centuries of Childhood,* traces the concept of childhood in France from medieval times, when children went straight into community life, where there was no time for solitude or privacy, through the eighteenth century, when bourgeois family households began to extend the notion – and practice – of privacy. Education was increasingly linked to moral education, and the development of schools effectively removed children from adult society. This has been a pervasive tendency in technocratic societies.

Similarly, de Beauvoir (1977) studied the images of old people in history and literature, noting a major distinction between technocratic and pre-technocratic societies. The first valorise youth, whereas the second, where life and work are more integrated, value the increased ability that comes with age. In industrialised societies, age can even be a kind of stigma, where the elderly are regarded as less useful or even useless, a burden rather than an asset in societies geared to economism and the devaluation of symbolic capital. The kind of social memory carried by elderly people is considered to be relatively unimportant to those concerned with technocratic know-how, speed and the production of material goods. As a result, old age has come to be defined as a medical problem – even, as de Beauvoir noted, a *disease.* Of course, there are wide variations. The elderly poor are generally less healthy and more bored, and meaningful activity, both physical and intellectual, is crucially important (see de Beauvoir, 1977; Matthews, 1979; Russell, 1981; Harichaux, Rougier and Palis, 1982). But we need to recognise that the physical cannot be separated from social, cultural and spiritual concerns, that an emphasis on the apparently 'natural' deterioration of bodies will tell us very little about ageing. Since ageing is also a social and cultural construct, it raises questions about the formation and maintenance of psycho-social identities and about specific cultural contexts.

These questions became particularly pertinent in the experience of migration. Basically, someone who migrates is carried across into a different state of being. Some of the Indian indentured labourers in Fiji and the Caribbean compared this experience to that of death, of being transported across the dark waters (Jayawardena, 1963). However benign the experience, migrants face a different language, different expectations and a new set of limitations – what the phenomenologist Alfred Schutz described as 'a labyrinth in which (the migrant) has lost all sense of his bearings' (Schutz, 1964, p.105). Migrant workers can to some extent define themselves as workers, and perhaps by focussing on their expectations for their children – usually the major reasons for migrating. But the elderly tend to be attached to the families of labour migrants or to have completed their own working lives. In a context defined by work, they frequently lead relatively idle and dependent existences. Even where their families are supportive and loving, their own symbolic capital is devalued in the new environment. Kinship and social networks have a narrower range, and the cultural capital acquired over a lifetime in one place dwindles to individual characteristics, or to the less differentiated status of being a parent or grandparent whose authority is not always supported and may even be undermined by the surrounding institutions of the new society. As we have seen in earlier chapters, the very status of 'migrantness' is often a negative one, marked by perceived linguistic deficiency and, in many cases, by relative poverty. It is worth reiterating at this point that economic, symbolic and cultural capital cannot be clearly separated, especially where 'success' is defined in economic terms and money can buy both services and relative independence.

Elsewhere, I have argued that these negative connotations of 'migrantness' can be partly resisted by more positive self-identifications derived from another cultural framework – for example, exploited migrant workers can still maintain some self-respect as honourable people or good parents within the terms of their own understandings of these qualities (see Bottomley, 1979, 1987). Such resistance is partly conscious and often articulated – by, for example, comparing the loose morals or selfish behaviour of members of the dominant group with one's own standards of proper conduct. But, as we have seen, cultural expectations and expressions are not always conscious. They are also embodied in habitus, through which the social world appears as a symbolic system, a space structured by different lifestyles and different schemes of perception and appreciation. Although there are always struggles over the power to produce and impose legitimate views of the world, habitus may be relatively unquestioned.

Migrants, therefore, not only consciously reconstruct practices and beliefs carried across with them, but also literally embody certain predispositions. Nevertheless, as we have seen in earlier chapters, these beliefs and practices must be negotiated in the new conditions and many are denied, devalued and distorted in the process. I would argue that some of the impact of this struggle is manifested physically; that one can, to some extent, 'read' the history of social and cultural encounters in bodily metaphors. For example, recent detailed studies of Greek-Australians indicate that as immigrants they become less healthy over the years. Part of the explanation of this decline in health is dietary – the consumption of more meat and more dairy products, fewer pulses, vegetables and, especially, fewer olives (see Powles, 1990). Clearly, an adjustment towards a more Anglo-Australian diet has negatively affected the health of these particular migrants. More obvious examples come from industrial health problems, such as accidents and repetitive strain injuries arising from the location of immigrants in the workforce.

As a result, elderly immigrants may have health problems *because* of migration. Their bodies have paid a high price for the move. At the same time, less obvious consequences can also link social and cultural circumstances with physical and psychological effects. The medical model concentrates on bodily symptoms, in terms of illness. But, as Susan Sontag and others have shown, illness can be a metaphor for much more complex processes (Sontag, 1978; Turner, 1987). The medical model can also be a form of domination in itself, a way of reducing someone to the status of a patient, literally waiting to be cared for.

This is more and more the case with old people. Defined as redundant because no longer useful in production or reproduction, they are frequently put aside – in homes, in corners, at the margins of social activity. For the aged migrant this kind of marginality compounds that created by migrantness and the isolation of language. Their infantilisation can be reinforced by having to rely on their offspring to interpret the world for them and, at times, by their economic and even physical dependence on their offspring.

At the same time, consumer societies stress youthfulness and people increasingly strive to look young. The various markers of age of less technocratic societies – such as the wearing of black or sombre colours – serve as diacritical features of difference in the new context.

DANCE, AGEING AND COMMUNICATION

In a number of ways, therefore, elderly people can become immobilised, by social, cultural and physical factors. Their immobilisation and relative powerlessness is also being resisted, particularly by those who have the means to confront political institutions. And, of course, some elderly men are extremely powerful, as the rulers of China have recently demonstrated. It is probably the case that access to economic, cultural and symbolic capital is most important in old age.

In countries like Greece, marginalisation of the elderly is less pronounced. In general, members of a family still retain some respect from, and interaction with younger members, despite considerable inroads into the older ideas of family honour. As I demonstrated in chapter 7, the family is still a central motif of Greek life, and elderly women are widely referred to as 'grandmothers', and often held in some awe. Beyond the family, however, many old people are isolated and lonely, left behind in nearly-deserted villages or city apartments. Over the last ten years or so, the Greek government has established Centres for the Protection of the Elderly (KAPI) throughout Greece, which provide day care facilities and activities of all kinds, from physiotherapy and health care to dancing, music groups and other creative endeavours. Some of the dance groups set up in these centres now perform at international festivals of dance.

I would like to trace this theme of dance once again, in relation to the issues of ageing, migrantness and habitus, outlined above. I mentioned in chapter 5 that almost everyone in Greece participates in the dance, at some time. In villages, children would learn to dance early by following their elders, and dancing might continue until people are literally too old to dance (two of the KAPI stars were in their 90s). There is nothing undignified about the dances, none of the 'mutton dressed as lamb' elements that might exclude older people. Nevertheless, as I demonstrated in chapter 5, the dances are both socially and sensually pleasurable.

In Greece, as elsewhere, dance is increasingly confined to the young, and increasingly dominated by disco or display of various kinds, or both. Even where village dances are performed, the performers are usually young, and the elderly are relegated to the audience. This is particularly true of Greek-Australians, who usually learn their dancing as part of a performance team attached to a Brotherhood or a community organisation. Older people do dance at family or other festivities, but their opportunities are relatively limited – by small and crowded dance floors, and by the need to travel for long distances in the congested cities in which most Greek-Australians live.

At the same time, the Greek-born population is ageing. By the year 2001, about 40 per cent will be over 60 years of age (A.I.M.A., 1985, p.21). This fact has been the subject of attention by numerous definers of social knowledge, including those policy makers and others who complain of the 'social burden' represented by the elderly. Several homes have been established for elderly people of non-English-speaking background, as well as ethno-specific health services (see McCallum, 1990). Once again, however, there is little attention being paid to what 'ethno-specific' might mean, apart from language. Language is crucially important, but a genuinely multicultural society would recognise that it is possible to learn more than languages from an immigrant population. As I argued in chapter 5, I believe that dance and music are muted modes that are too often not heard – or, more precisely, not listened to in countries of immigration like Australia. The African Americans have made their music and dance an international phenomenon – and, in many cases, a highly commercial one. But there are other ways of recognising and learning from the symbolic capital that is brought from another place and, too often, squandered. Dance is an example of such capital – like Attali, quoted in chapter 5, we could try to 'hear' the circle dance.

In the context of ageing and migrantness, dance can have a particular significance. It can have cathartic effects, as a number of writers have noted (for example, Raftis, 1983; Spencer, 1985). In personal terms, the euphoria of dance can help to dissolve some of the tensions and contradictions that arise from the experience of migration. It can also help in reasserting identity – as a Greek, or as someone from a particular region or village. What Erikson calls 'psychosocial identity' is constructed in a particular place and time. Although identities develop and change, a stable basis is important as a touchstone for such changes (Erikson, 1968). Collective participation in activities such as Greek dance can reactivate the earlier bases of identity formation. In fact, dance can stimulate memory in a particularly evocative way. A Limnian woman in her mid-sixties once confided to me that she felt that she was not dancing in the rather bare hall in Sydney, but 'at home', in her village, as a young girl. She told me that she could 'even smell the pine trees'. A younger man, who gave up teaching dance performance groups in order to continue his own (superb) dancing for pleasure, also said that this pleasure was partly the feeling of 'connecting' with his youth in

Greece, where, in a milieu of fairly poor Pontian refugees, people of all ages would gather outside their small houses, talk and joke together, play the *lyra*, sing, dance and forget their hunger and fatigue.

This kind of embodiment of memory can work powerfully against the silencing that marks both migration and ageing. In his book, *The Body and Society* (1986) Bryan Turner has suggested that industrial societies emphasise 'closed bodies'. Emotion and intimacy are limited to privacy, and the 'public' is defined by formality. Hence bodies in industrial societies are more closed than in those places where bodies are more overtly linked to the public world, for example in ritual and carnival. In Greece, communal dance has always been part of the annual ritual cycle, marking feast days and public festivals, as well as Carnival and Easter celebrations, in a shared and public symbolic space.

There are important aspects of Greek dance that support the idea of an opening out of the personal to the social. One of those is in memory and psycho-social identity, as I have suggested above. Another is a kind of conversation in dance; the dancers communicate with each other and with the music in a language that resonates with memory and habitus. There is an order of dancing, a way of dancing, of holding hands, of recognising other dancers and the musicians. There is also the physical contact with others and the pervasive and sensual effect of the music. The collective euphoria of dance and the repetition of phrases and steps can even induce a trance-like state (see Raftis, 1983). The overall effect can certainly be one of *exstasis*, literally lifting the dancers out of their individual everyday realities. It can also be *kefi*, a collective heightening of emotion that is shared pleasure (see chapter 5).

Specifically, in relation to elderly Greek-Australians, I believe that dance can offer much more than just exercise. It can provide the kind of conversation described above, as well as an affirmation of socio-cultural identity, formed in the pre-migration habitus, but also affected by the experience of migration and of minority status. Some Greek community workers in Sydney have begun to encourage elderly people to dance, with considerable success. Not only has their physical mobility improved as a result, but their self-confidence and openness has also increased. One of these groups has carefully created their own costumes and accepted invitations to perform at several functions. Increasingly confident of their own memories of dance, they have also consulted a dance teacher to help them with the elaborations (*figures*) that mark the more accomplished dancers. Not only are they using some of their devalued knowledge and experience – their symbolic capital; they are also keen to develop it. This celebration of their cultural memories is by no means a retreat to ethnicity: it is a positive statement of another way of becoming old.

CHAPTER 9

Intersections:
gender, ethnicity, class and culture in Australia

Never in the history of Australia have so many streams
flowed: if we have parched and desiccated minds and spirits,
the fault is our own . . . There is nothing that engenders and
nourishes fear like ignorance, and with it the threat to my
status, my group, my understanding of the matter.
McCaughey, 1988, p.2

The themes discussed throughout this book have a particular
significance in the context of a country of immigration, such as
Australia. The specific ways in which economies, policies and
existing cultural forms define the lives of migrants reveal important
similarities and differences within a society. Analyses of these can
demonstrate some of the constitutive social processes that we refer
to by abstractions such as 'class', 'ethnicity', 'gender' and even 'nation'.

Such analyses are by definition critical, in bringing into question
some of the hallowed ideals of most countries of immigration – ideals
such as democracy, freedom, tolerance and equality before the law.
Critics of multiculturalism in Australia sometimes suggest that this
challenging of ideals in the name of representation weakens the
ideals themselves. Others, including myself, believe that the gaps
revealed between theory and practice are in themselves far more
destructive of such valuable and civilised principles.

Several writers have critically explored some of the implications
of immigration in relation to nationalism and Australian identity
(see, for example, Bottomley, 1988; Castles, et al. 1988; Pettman, 1988;
de Lepervanche, 1990; Turpin, 1990). However, it is fair to say that
immigration, despite its centrality to Australian history, has been
surprisingly ignored in the writing of that history. The establishment of colonies, and subsequent migration of British and Irish
settlers, are systematically included in 'Australian history', but
the massive immigration of non-Anglophone people, especially

following the introduction of a mass migration program in 1947, is generally subsumed under studies of migrants, ethnics and multiculturalism. For example, a recent report on the teaching of Australian studies in tertiary education (CRASTE, 1987) virtually ignored non-Anglophone people, but included a section on multiculturalism that concentrated on a kind of museum function, of conserving and documenting the cultural heritage of ethnic minorities. An alternative approach had been suggested in a thoughtful submission from the Australian Greek Welfare Society, who proposed an integration of 'value positions derived from other cultures into Australian Studies and *all other studies*' (p.95) – in other words, a real recognition of diversity and of Australian cultures as dynamic and interactive.

Such a recognition would certainly reflect the statistical and social realities of Australia, where more than four out of ten residents (about six million people) are direct products of the post-war migration program (Collins, 1988, p.10). Despite this, the perspective suggested by the Australian Greek Welfare Society will continue to be resisted by those whose cultural capital is invested in Anglomorphism, for reasons that are mainly political, having to do with the legitimate control of knowledge and the protection of 'authority'.

I suggested in earlier chapters that intellectual frameworks can help to maintain the control of knowledge by means of schemata based on dichotomies – for example, between public–private, male–female, economy–culture, and so on. Disciplinary boundaries can have a similar effect, excluding certain subject matter as 'out of place' (as non-Anglophones are apparently out of place in Australian history). This means that entire discourses can proceed without reference to each other, although the reality of social experience is one of constant interaction, as we have seen in discussions of migration and cultural change (chapters 2 and 3), and of gender in relation to religion, the economy, political movements and the ethnos in Greece (chapter 7).

In this chapter, I plan to demonstrate some of these interactions in the Australian context, organising material around the themes of class, ethnicity and gender; not serially, but attempting to interrelate the three. At the same time, I am concerned with particular discourses in, for example, feminist, Marxist and ethnicist writings as well as those of migration studies. My perspective here is mostly structural, demonstrating some of the ways in which people's lives are defined, limited and altered by migration, by economic and employment possibilities, by gender relations and by state policies and practices. I would prefer to include in this account more about people's perceptions of these structures. As I mentioned in chapters 1 and 8, when discussing Bourdieu's notion of habitus, we also need to recognise that social reality is an object of perception. However, I know from earlier studies of subjectivities how specific and detailed such work has to be (Bottomley, 1979, 1983). In this chapter, I will make some suggestions about ways people perceive the structures discussed, based mainly on long-term observation and discussion, and on earlier studies. Literary sources are also a way into subjectivities, as we saw in chapters 4 and 8. But a deeper understanding of the effects of some of the structures and events discussed here would require closer attention to their interpretation by the 'subjects' themselves. Once again, I will be discussing Greek-Australians, partly because an ethno-specific study has greater rigour than a more general survey of migrants or non-Anglophones. It will also be valuable to relate this material to earlier references to Greece and Greek-Australians.

INTERCONNECTIONS

Anthias and Yuval-Davis (1983) offered useful suggestions for studying the intersection of ethnicity, gender and class, rather than concentrating on one or the other and assuming the homogeneity of each category. In context, one of these may be more salient than another, but each differs with respect to the other perspectives. For example, they suggest that gender divisions are more important than ethnic divisions in employment. But gender definitions differ according to ethnicity, and the control of reproduction can be a means of both ethnic and class subordination. Thus:

> ... virtually everywhere the interests of the nation or the ethnic group are seen as those of its male subjects, and the interests of the state are endowed with those of a male ethnic class and not just a class which is 'neutral' in terms of ethnicity and gender ... At the same time, women of dominant ethnic groups are often in a position to control the reproductive role of women of other ethnic groups by state welfare and legal policies, as well as to use them as servants and child minders in order to ease part of their own reproductive burden. (Anthias and Yuval Davis, 1983, p.71)

Moreover, some ethnic families use the labour of their women as an economic resource in a way that may be perfectly acceptable within the ethnic framework, but can mean considerable exploitation of women, and sometimes of children. But, as we will see later, it can also lead to economic success in the country of settlement.

Differentiation within each of these categories tends to be ignored or elided. As Anthias and Yuval-Davis point out, analyses based on class usually neglect women and minorities and those based on ethnicity tend to disregard women and class. I have already discussed some of these absences in previous chapters, where we saw some of the ways in which ethnicities are cross-cut by class and gender differences. Anthias and Yuval-Davis criticise ethnocentrism in feminist analyses, which also have a pervasive middle-class bias and, at times, a somewhat reductionist view of family life. The debate generated by their paper continued in subsequent issues of *Feminist Review*, including contributions by Barrett and McIntosh (1985), Ramazanoglu (1986), Lees (1986) and Parmar (1989).

Other British writers have, in fact, shown considerable sensitivity to the intersection of these three perspectives. In a collection called *The Empire Strikes Back*, Hazel Carby, whose chapter title is 'White Woman Listen!', calls into question many of the feminist assumptions about liberation, and the view that black women entering Britain are moving into greater emancipation. She also argues that women of immigrant minorities are frequently reduced to a category such as 'Asian' or 'Caribbean' or even 'migrant women' and that their specific experiences and resistances are ignored (Carby, 1982).

In another chapter in the same collection, Pratibha Parmar writes about Asian women's resistance to various forms of oppression, challenging commonsense images of Asian women as docile and politically inert (Parmar, 1982). She points out that some of the criteria used for political action (such as membership of unions) neglects the migrants' experiences of unions in Britain and in their countries of origin, where they were often 'instruments of management' (p.263). In fact, Parmar demonstrates, Asian women have been at the fore in several key industrial struggles in Britain over the last decade, as well as in countries such as Korea and Malaysia (Parmar, 1982).

Another excellent collection of British material was edited by Annie Phizacklea under the title of *One Way Ticket: Migration and Female Labour* (1983). It includes studies of second-generation West Indian, Greek-Cypriot and Turkish women, women workers and transnational production, motherhood and waged work, providing an excellent example of the combination of the three perspectives of ethnicity, gender and class. The paper by Floya Anthias traces very clearly experiences of Greek-Cypriot women, 'whose labour is used as the cornerstone of the Greek-Cypriot ethnic economy in Britain' (p.75). Women are the mainstay of the clothing industry, susceptible to high unemployment and low job security. The industry has a marked sexual division of labour, with men much more likely to be employers. At the same time, the sexual division of domestic labour leaves women solely responsible for child care and housework, sustaining the family form that defines Greek-Cypriot social life, but without the degree of support or of leisure that might be available in Cyprus itself (Anthias, 1983).

THE AUSTRALIAN CONTEXT

In Australia, there have been several attempts to integrate these three sets of issues, but these have met with some resistance, or a form of studied neglect, perhaps because all three are foci of political mobilisation and act as boundary markers. My own accounts of Greek-Australian women (1974, 1975, 1979, 1980, 1983, 1984a and 1984c) seem to have made little impact on feminists, class analysts or ethnicists, who mostly remain focussed on one or the other perspective. 'Migrant women' (a catch-all category concealing multiple differences) were for some time subsumed as the families of migrants. Workers were deemed to be male, and the task of these families was partly to preserve ethnic traditions, as well as to stabilise the private sphere of life, which was seen as unquestionably separate from the public sphere of work and political activity, as in the model Parsonian family. The effects of the wider society and the dynamics of cultural processes, including those of class and gender, were left unquestioned (cf. Zubrzycki, 1978).

Some of the more ethnographic studies paid specific attention to women – and indeed were undertaken by women: Martin, *Refugee Settlers* (1965), Huber, *From Pasta to Pavlova* (1977), Bottomley, *After the Odyssey* (1979), for example. These studies raised questions about the separation of the private and the public, demonstrating that particular forms of economic activities had specific consequences for migrant families. For example, in Huber's study, Trevisani immigrants living in the agricultural area of Griffith, New South Wales, could maintain something like the extended families of Treviso, whereas families settling in Leichhardt, Sydney, and working as individual industrial labourers had more nucleated households and were more isolated from kin and friends.

In 1974, I published a paper comparing 'sex roles' among Greek Australians with those represented in material about Greece. One of the conclusions was that women who shared the ownership and management of small businesses in Sydney had a stronger sense of independence and a greater part in decision-making than those who remained dependent on their husbands' earnings. In other words, economic participation partly determined gender relations.

A year later, I contributed a short piece about migrant women to a book about women in Australia (Mercer, 1975). My chapter, also based on fieldwork in Sydney, focussed on the contrast between pre-migration and post-migration experiences of women from villages. It discussed how the overlapping of social spheres in rural Greece had created what (following Geertz) I called 'centripetal forces' that maintained women at the centre of important activities to do with kinship, religion, networks of friends, the education of children and, quite often, with production. Once these rural families migrated to urban Australia – or the U.S.A. or Canada – family members were likely to be 'spun off' as individuals, to work as labourers, to study at state-run schools at a distance from home, to attend church services in another suburb, and so on. I argued that these 'centrifugal' tendencies isolated women, especially mothers, in something of a vacuum, as they had lost a good deal of control over the activities of the family and, with it, a sense of positive identity as wives and mothers.

The 1975 paper was not well received. The most vocal feminists at that time were less than enthusiastic about the virtues of motherhood and the family and were also probably even less aware then than now of the complexities of ethnocentrism in feminist writing. Moreover, the chapter was published at the same time as an excellent study of migrant women workers in industry that concentrated on their often appalling conditions of work (Storer, 1976). My short piece had not stressed the working conditions of the women about whom I wrote, although it did cover the problems of shift work and of long hours of heavy work outside the home added to domestic labour. This experience was quite familiar to me, not only in the lives of the southern European women I knew, but in the life of my own mother, who worked overlong days in exploitative conditions and returned to the domestic chores in the evening. The southern European women had the additional problems of language and unfamiliarity with their new country. My mother could be exploited as a single parent without educational qualifications, in a country town where jobs were scarce and unions virtually non-existent. Perhaps that personal experience allowed me to understand the need to make connections between 'home' and 'work' rather than to analyse them separately. It also helps me to be wary of concentration on one sphere of existence or one perspective of understanding.

The very harshness and the structured unfreedom of my mother's conditions made it even more important for her to strive to be a good mother and a decent woman. This is also true for many migrant women I know, whose sparkling houses and carefully-fed children reveal a kind of resistance to oppression – in Bourdieu's terms, a recourse to available symbolic capital. As I suggested in chapter 7 above, when discussing Muriel Dimen's account of the domestic work of women in Epiros, these efforts may be over-determined and oppressive in themselves, but they have considerable significance for the women who make them. Some of the early feminist responses were somewhat monistic in their efforts to resist what were seen as traditional definitions of 'women's roles'. The other more 'labourist' orientation was not dissociated, in that women were seen primarily as workers, with additional problems arising from gender – such as the need for child care, and the burden of a double workload. Politically, however, this latter orientation has been very important and has served to reveal the central part played by migrant women in the development of Australian manufacturing industries. Some unions have taken up the cause of migrant women workers, but the decline in the economy has actually worsened conditions for many.

Nevertheless, much of the feminists' and political economists' writings tended to blur 'migrant women' into a category, defined by patriarchal oppressions on the one hand and harsh working conditions, on the other. Several women from the Italian workers' organisation, FILEF, took exception to some of these assumptions, pointing out that Italian women, defined as politically inactive in Australia, were impeded by their class position as immigrant workers, rather than by their supposedly macho men or patriarchal traditions. In Italy, of course, women are politically active as feminists and industrial workers (Sgro, Pieri and Risk, 1980). Following this argument, I have compared the differences between the women's movements and political action in Greece and Australia, noting that women's politics have been closely tied to left-wing politics in Greece, whereas 'Australian women, who gained the vote 46 years before their Greek sisters, are still struggling for recognition within male-dominated political parties' (Bottomley, 1984a, p.108).

I might have added that women of non-Anglophone background were – and are still – struggling for recognition by their Anglo-Australian sisters. In 1984, I was invited by feminists in Greece to a conference of Mediterranean Women's Organisations, held in Delphi. My paper at that conference provided an account of the lives of Mediterranean women in Australia, discussing employment, health, sexual harassment, family life and feminist and state initiatives (see Bottomley, 1984c). One of the editors of a book about Australian women, who read this paper, asked if it could be included in the forthcoming publication. Some months later, she explained that it had to be excluded to make room for papers more relevant to feminists. At the last minute, apparently in response to some criticisms of ethnocentrism, she asked if I could write a 'more general paper about migrant women'.

I referred her to Jeannie Martin, who provided an interesting chapter on non-English-speaking women, which raised important issues about these three perspectives (Martin, 1986) and reiterated some of the arguments she had put forward in the collection *Ethnicity, Class and Gender in Australia* (Bottomley and de Lepervanche, 1984).

Basically, Jeannie Martin's argument was that the mass migration program in Australia represented a need for labour and for consumers; hence the policy of settler migration rather than 'guest workers'. Although women were brought to Australia mainly as dependants (wives, daughters, sisters and mothers) of male workers, they were also over-represented as workers, especially in the first ten years of arrival. 'Between 1970 and 1980 workforce participation rates among newly arrived immigrant women ranged between 50% and 85%' (Martin, 1984, p.112). The majority of these women were married with young children, creating what she describes as 'a tension between production and social reproduction' that was compounded by expectations from countries of origin, of the central significance of women's tasks as mothers and wives (p.113). Martin notes that the dichotomies production–consumption, public–private and work–non-work falsify the constant interaction between these supposedly separate spheres. She also comments on the ways in which the one, more valued – and more male-dominated sphere – dominates and transforms the other. For example, 'working effectively in consumption almost always involves having to work in production, particularly if the wage coming into the household is inadequate for family survival' (p.120). According to Martin, the Marxist literature on Australian immigration is 'singularly productionist in nature', considering migrant women as 'honorary males or a subcategory of male' (p.121).

Other contributions to *Ethnicity, Class and Gender in Australia* (Bottomley and de Lepervanche, 1984) covered a number of important topics related to the title of the book. These included a study of Lebanese families confronting the disjunction between Australian family law and Islamic law (Humphrey); the intersection of ethnicity, gender and class in the lives of Sicilian-Australians (Hampel), the stigma of 'migrantness', with particular reference to health practices (Morrissey), and a critique of the sociobiological justification of inequalities in terms of their 'naturalness' (de Lepervanche). This book, which was in press when the article by Anthias and Yuval-Davis was published, raised similar critiques of unidimensional approaches. Since then, several of the authors have taken their analyses further in a book entitled *Intersexions: Gender/Class/Culture/Ethnicity* (Bottomley et al., 1991), which takes into account more recent feminist and post-colonial critiques of dominant discourses. Yuval-Davis and Anthias have also developed their earlier framework in an excellent volume, *Woman–Nation–State* (1989). I will return to these developments later, after analysis of some of the inter-referencing of class, ethnicity, gender and culture in the lives of Greek-Australians.

THE LIMITS OF NECESSITY

At the 1986 census, over 20 per cent of Australia's population had been born outside the country. Of those, perhaps one quarter came from countries around the Mediterranean. The largest number were Italian-born (262,000) and the next were Greek-born (138,000) (DILGEA, quoted in Castles et al., p.19). Melbourne is frequently cited as the third largest Greek city in the world. Within the Greek population, as we saw in chapter 5, there is an economic distinction between pre-war and post-war migrants, in that the former generally set up their own businesses, and the latter were more likely to be industrial workers. In 1947, 71.6 per cent of Greek-born men were working in the catering industry, mostly as business proprietors (Price, 1968, quoted in Bottomley, 1979, p.45). Greeks are still well represented as self-employed, but the picture is fairly complex. According to a recent study in Sydney, Greek men were almost twice as likely as other men and Greek women almost three times as likely as other women to be self-employed (Tait and Gibson, 1987, p.15). At the same time, 27 per cent of Greek-born men and 28.1 per cent of Greek-born women were employed as labourers and factory workers, compared with 7.3 per cent and 18.6 per cent respectively for Australian-born men and women (ibid., p.11, Table 4 and p.12, Table 5). And the category of 'self-employed' can include such marginal employment as outwork, which I will discuss later.

Partly because of their positive emphasis on education, Greek-speakers are over-represented in tertiary education and have produced a large number of bilingual professional people whose presence often belies the genuine hardships faced by many first-generation immigrants. In fact, opportunity has been highly structured by the specific economic circumstances in Australia at the time of migration. Since the mid-1970s, the decline in manufacturing and the inter-nationalisation of industries producing clothing, footwear and whitegoods has resulted in the loss of thousands of jobs in which Mediterranean migrants were concentrated. In 1984, 13.2 per cent of Greek-born workers and 18.2 per cent of Yugoslav-born workers were unemployed. The figures are even worse for immigrants born in Lebanon (32.1 per cent) and Vietnam (32.7 per cent) (Tait and Gibson, 1987, p.8, Table 2 – figures are for workers arriving after 1960 aged 18 or over).

As we have seen, both men and women were brought to Australia as workers and consumers. In 1975, 45 per cent of women born in Italy and 56 per cent of women born in Greece worked as labourers, production or process workers (Storer, 1976). Greek- and Italian-born women, particularly, were also concentrated in the clothing industry. With the decline of that industry, these women (together with Turkish, Latin-American, and Asian migrants) have moved increasingly into outwork, often working at home, without union coverage, at wages well below that of factory workers. According to a recent study, outworkers may be paid as little as 50 cents for a pair of pyjamas, and 80 cents for a dress (Centre for Working Women, 1986).

In a way, the growth of outwork is symptomatic of the various structured limitations on the lives of these women. They are forced into the work by the need to sustain themselves and their families and by the relative absence of adequate child care facilities. Outwork conflates production and social reproduction, without the compensations available to 'real' workers – such as sick pay, holiday pay, award conditions and safety regulations – but with the additional burdens of domestic workers, such as preparing meals and supervising children. In the study undertaken by the Centre for Working Women in Melbourne, many outworkers complained of intimidation by the middlemen who delivered their work. Some of these men were violent and some delivered materials late at night and sexually harassed the women, especially single mothers. Workers were also constrained by their lack of knowledge of English, by a cultural resistance to factory work, and by the need to care for elderly relatives as well as children. The worsening labour market is also important, and in the report by the Centre for Working Women it is argued that employers are deliberately choosing outwork to reduce overheads and increase profit (1986, pp.8–9). Not surprisingly, exploitative working conditions such as these have caused widespread health problems. A recent study of 50 Greek households in Marrickville, Sydney, revealed that 40 per cent of households had experienced work-related illness of one or more members (Bottomley and Georgiou, 1988). The 1976 report on migrant women in industry mentioned repetitive strain injuries, back problems, varicose veins and constant headaches among workers (Storer, 1976). Later studies show these and other stress-related illnesses to be a continuing problem for Mediterranean workers (see Jakubowicz et al., 1984).

At the same time, they have been confronted by institutions and practitioners constructed by and for the English-speaking population and usually well trained in ethnocentrism. We will see later just how far this training can go! For the present, it is worth noting that workers of non-Anglo-Celtic background are often the victims of a form of racism, are less likely to win compensation cases and more likely to be labelled as malingerers or neurotics (cf. Morrissey, 1984). There have even been reported cases of non-English-speaking women being prescribed the dangerous contraceptive DepoProvera because it is easy to administer (Bottomley, 1984c). In my research in the early seventies, I also heard of doctors who were prescribing cortisone for the children of anxious Mediterranean mothers who thought that their children were underweight (cortisone, potentially lethal, giving patients an artificially plump, rosy appearance). Several doctors were later de-registered as a result of this practice.

The point I am making here is that the working conditions and economic circumstances of these immigrants makes the analytic separation of work and non-work, or production and consumption, quite unviable. Obviously these conditions affect health, happiness and family life. To some extent, many Mediterranean families have resisted the individualising of industrial work by working as families. This is still arduous, but it has enabled some sharing and even some cushioning of family members in times of hardship. These enterprises show quite clearly the overlap of production and social reproduction and, while women still work double shifts in these arrangements, they may also have some economic leverage as partners in family businesses. In a study I made in 1973, I found a degree of interdependence in such families that was lacking in those where women were financially dependent on their husbands (Bottomley, 1974). This finding is similar to that of Sutton in Athens, who argues that the more domesticated women in her sample were also more marginalised in family decision-making (1986).

It is clear that economic conditions structure family life and social relations. In chapter 6, I described the practice of dowry as a means of maintaining family status. Investment in education also reflects positively on the whole family and may be the outcome of con- siderable sacrifice, especially by parents. Many children recognise this sacrifice and regard educational success as something of an obligation, even if they resent it at times. Greek-Australian secondary and university students have told me stories of the hardships suffered by their parents and expressed their own determination to make these efforts worthwhile (Bottomley, 1979, 1983). At the other extreme, however, are children who take on the racism of the playground or the wider environment and see their parents as 'stupid peasants' or 'just factory workers' who cannot speak English properly and exhibit shameful differences in behaviour. This kind of perception comes through in migrant writing (such as the example I have offered in chapter 8), but also in some women's accounts of their own experiences. It is often exacerbated when parents are forced to use their children as interpreters, thus reversing the parent–child roles and heightening the parents' own feelings of inadequacy.

We can see therefore that the public and private spheres are by no means separate, especially for people whose social space is so pre-determined by economic and political structures. In fact, the ability to delineate a private sphere is an attribute of social power. For the relatively powerless, private space may be minimal. Labour migrants, therefore, are defined by their foreignness as well as by economic conditions that delimit the range of available possibilities. I have argued here and elsewhere that cultural and symbolic capital provides some resources, especially for people who retain a positive sense of their collective traditions. But it is important to recognise the extent to which objective necessity structures lifestyles.

STATE INTERVENTION AND THE BOUNDARIES OF 'THE PRIVATE'

In a basic sense, the very presence of migrants in Australia is a state concern. The migration program is an outcome of Federal govern-ment policy and a topic of constant debate across the political spectrum. The restriction on non-white immigration (the so-called White Australia policy) reflected not only notions of racial purity and white superiority that harked back to European imperialism, but, at the same time, protectionist views of workers who were unwilling to lose hard-won conditions (Curthoys and Markus, 1978).

The post-war program focussed on labour migration as an essential component for the development of Australian capitalism. The program has always been carefully controlled by the Federal government with an eye for labour shortages, sexual imbalances, and racial mix. An attack by a Melbourne history professor, Geoffrey Blainey, on what he called 'the Asianisation of Australia' generated a political debate that culminated in the replacement of the then Minister for Immigration by a more conservative Minister and a more restrictionist policy. I do not intend to discuss immigration policy here, since the subject has been well covered elsewhere (see Martin, 1978; de Lepervanche, 1984b; Jakubowicz, 1984; Markus and Ricklefs, 1985). For the purposes of this chapter, it is enough to note that the lives of migrants have been significantly formed by government policy, which defines conditions of eligibility for entry to Australia, access to work, provision of facilities such as schools, child care centres, English language classes, hospitals and public transport. By comparison with many other countries of immigration, the Australian state assumes a heavy responsibility for migrants, partly because of the policy of settler migration which, unlike guest-worker policies elsewhere, implies some responsibility for social reproduction. At the same time, those companies who have made enormous profits from migrant labour have not been required to make provision for their workers, as they have in some European countries (cf. Castles and Kosack, 1973).

The first wave of post-war migrants, mainly refugees from eastern Europe, were often sent under contract to work in state-financed development programs such as the Snowy River Scheme. They usually worked as labourers, although many were highly qualified tradesmen and professionals. Other labour migrants were brought to fill specific vacancies in manufacturing industries. The outcome of this program has been a concentration of non-English-speaking migrants in particular occupations and, by association, in particular segments of the workforce, as well as certain residential areas. For these people, the limits of necessity were largely defined by state policy. At the same time, Australia's interventionist state, by comparison with the U.S.A., for example, has followed a largely social democratic welfare program. Some of the services funded by the Commonwealth government over the last 35 years have included the provision of migrant hostels, the Adult Migrant English Service, grants to community agencies, the Child Migrant Education program, English and community education programs on television, the Telephone Interpreter Service, bilingual welfare officers, ethnic radio and access radio, and ethnic television. In addition, four States have set up their own Ethnic Affairs Commissions, which carry out research and community education projects, liaise with government departments and ethnic organisations and provide language services such as interpreting and translating. The Federal and State branches of the Department of Immigration and Ethnic Affairs also have bilingual advisors, as do a range of government departments, such as Social Security, Youth and Community Services, Education and Health. There are also bodies of appeal, such as Equal Opportunity Boards, Anti-Discrimination Boards, Workers' Compensation Commissions and special Women's Co-ordination units. A Women's Desk was established in the Department of Immigration and Ethnic Affairs in 1983.

The authors of a recent report on ethnicity, class and social policy in Australia point out that the welfare state stresses equity and justice in an attempt to guarantee a basic quality of life. But the state is also crucially concerned with the reproduction of social relations and with social control. According to these authors, the latter concerns have taken priority in Australia (Jakubowicz et al., 1984). Jean Martin, analysing institutional responses to the migrant presence in Australia in 1977, made the point that

Whether naturalised or not, immigrants are peculiarly subject to control by the state in that their freedom to establish a family unit is limited by the state's power to decide what other family members may join them as settlers in Australia. (1978, p.18)

Martin examined the link between knowledge and power and the construction of legitimate knowledge about immigrants. The policy of assimilation presented immigrants as invisible, although migrants themselves resisted and many returned home. As we saw in chapter 4, the 'problems' of immigrants were also attributed to their ethnicity or culture, rather than to economic or gender inequalities. The Whitlam Labor government (1972–75) was the first to explain these problems in terms of poverty and isolation, and initiatives of that government supported action by ethnic organisations concerned with participation and ethnic rights. After the overthrow of the Whitlam government, however, conservative policy was based on 'the active use of social policy initiatives to reinforce the power and the status of the more conservative and economically dominant elements of Australian society' (Jakubowicz et al., 1984, p.69). Since that time, social policy has generally ignored the economic bases of inequality, re-asserted the domination of the Immigration Department and specified the ethnic bourgeoisies as the legitimate mediators between government and people, defining an ethnic group model of organisations, for access to services.

The concern for social control has surfaced in some extremely oppressive forms. One of these was the deportation in 1977 of an organiser of the Italian workers' association, FILEF, who was active in advocating social and welfare rights among the Italian population of Melbourne. Another involved a witch hunt of massive proportions among the Greek population of Sydney, purportedly to investigate welfare fraud. This scandalous operation entailed dawn raids by Commonwealth police on the homes of Greek patients of doctors suspected of the fraud. Some 184 people were arrested and bundled into prison cells with drug addicts and other prisoners. Non-English-speakers were given no explanation of the purpose of the raids. Later, 763 invalid pensioners with Greek names had their benefits suspended, sometimes for months. One hundred and five of these were living in Greece, and my own contact with staff of International Social Services in Athens revealed at least two deaths as a result of those suspensions.

In Australia as well, the consequences for Greek families were devastating. Suicides and long-term traumas have been reported. One psychiatrist was actually arrested along with patients who were undergoing group therapy. The Crown case against all these people took four years to hear and cost perhaps ten million dollars – subsequent estimates have put the figure much higher (cf. the SBS film *Witchhunt*, 1988). The outcome has been that all charges have now been dismissed. Moreover, revelations about the procedures of the Department of Social Security and the confectionery evidence of the Commonwealth police are more reminiscent of Nazi Germany than of a quiet and supposedly egalitarian country such as Australia. Greeks used to dictatorships and military occupation certainly recognised the tactics used, but their personal experiences of oppression probably made this outrage even more painful. The Greek population responded with appropriate anger at the abuses of civil liberties and the slur cast on all Greek-Australians, most of whom value their reputations as hardworking and committed citizens of Australia. In our interviews with Greek householders in Marrickville, Vasilis Georgiou and I found that most respondents saw this case as an example of overt discrimination and a blow to the reputations of all Greeks. Almost every interviewee knew someone who had been questioned by police or had suffered the suspension of pension payments. Although the social security case was not widely publicised in the formal media, knowledge of the sorry details of the affair was obviously widespread (Bottomley and Georgiou, 1988). There is no doubt that such mass raids could not have been made on English or American migrants, or on super-wealthy Anglophone tax avoiders (who *do* exist). The evidence suggests that this was a lesson to discourage 'ethnics' from the potential misuse of the welfare system. Clearly, the provision of state welfare programs is only part of the story about the limitations on privacy. The social security witchhunt is an extreme case of state incursions, but intervention occurs daily and is obscured by the rhetoric of 'public–private'. Christopher Lasch (1979) and Jacques Donzelot (1979) have both written incisive studies of the policing of families by the law, the so-called helping professions and the knowledge industry, and by the incursions made by the spirit of the market place into the most personal of relations.

At a day-to-day level, migrants and members of ethnic minorities interact more often with bureaucrats than other members of the population. I have, for instance, cited the high unemployment figures among some migrant groups. Unemployment necessitates registration with the Commonwealth Employment Service and the Department of Social Security. Similarly, public health services are widely used by members of ethnic minorities, many of whom are also pensioners (welfare recipients) – because of illness, disability, single parent status, etc. Although interpreters are now more widely available, the staff of public institutions are rarely trained to cope with non-English-speakers and to take account of different cultural expectations. The result is often a form of racism that seems to have strengthened as the economy declines and the pressure on staff mounts. A report detailing discrimination against migrants by staff of the Department of Community Services and Health was not published or distributed by the Department (*Sydney Morning Herald*, February 4, 1988). The authors of the report claimed that migrant women were being particularly disadvantaged by the Department's lack of concern with reports of domestic violence, child care needs and the problems of the disabled, sick and elderly. Increasingly, women are being asked to take up the slack as the state reduces its funding of services.

RESISTANCES AND TRANSFORMATIONS

I have already discussed some forms of resistance to the limits of necessity. Material from earlier chapters even suggests that Greeks, for example, could have particular access to forms of resistance that give them a cultural advantage over many Anglo-Australians, despite the disadvantages of ethnic minority status and class location. One such strength lies in the kind of communalism that mobilised Greek speakers during the social security case. Greeks have also set up a large number of formal organisations in Australia, beginning with the establishment of the Greek Orthodox Community of New South Wales in 1899. In the early seventies, some 169 Greek organisations were counted in N.S.W. alone (Bottomley, 1979). In Victoria, there are probably more, one being the Australian Greek Welfare Society, which has played an important part in the campaign for ethnic rights and participation in the wider political sphere.

Jakubowicz has argued that neo-conservative strategies in Australia have incorporated and de-fused potential resistances by co-opting the leaders of ethnic organisations (1984). In the process, workers and women have been further marginalised. Some organisations, such as the Australian Greek Welfare Society and, especially, FILEF, have put considerable effort into action on behalf of workers and women (see chapter 8). But the emphasis on ethnicity in the policy of multiculturalism has played down class-based inequalities, and women are defined as auxiliaries in most community organisations.

In chapter 4 it was noted that structured inequalities in Australia were more likely to be based on class and gender than on ethnicity, and that Anglophone women, for example, were relatively powerless compared with Anglophone men. Australia has a pronounced sexual division of labour, and R. W. Connell estimates that the average income of women in Australia is 45 per cent of the average income of men (1987, p.7). Moreover, although women make up half the population, they formed only 9 per cent of elected representatives in State and Federal parliaments in 1984 (p.15).

In the case of migrant women, the pervasive sexism of Australian society may be compounded by specific cultural practices that derive from their countries of origin. At the considerable risk of echoing the very ethnocentrism I have criticised, I have to say that, on the basis of studies such as those of Gorecki (1987) and Humphrey (1984), and on the kind of evidence presented in chapter 7, patriarchalism is more in question in Australia than in many of the countries of origin of Australia's immigrants. A number of commentators have also noted that migrants are often more socially conservative in countries of immigration. Michael Kakakios and John van der Velden claim that the hegemonic form of Greekness in Australia stresses petit bourgeois values of economic success, the family as a primary form of social identity and loyalty, and patron–client relations (1984, p.150). One could add to these the emphasis on the 'good behaviour' of women and girls as the repositories of family honour (cf. Strintzos, 1984). Second generation Greek- and Italian-Australians remark on the difference between their parents' restrictiveness and the relative permissiveness they encounter on visits to Greece and Italy (cf. Bottomley, 1983, 1984a). Kakakios and van der Velden define these socially conservative tendencies as ideological, related to petit bourgeois dominance of ethnic organisations and 'community' representation. I believe they also have to do with the kind of 'fixing' of time that often occurs in migration, and with a desire to be respectable, in the absence of other forms of cultural and symbolic capital in a new and ethnocentric society.

Nevertheless, as we have seen, these models of tradition often fail to incorporate significant elements of change, such as the impact of women's movements in countries of origin. Moreover, the formal emphasis on ethnicity as a mode of organisation can lead to a restoration of superseded models of tradition, or, an emphasis on some diacritical features rather than others. Thus, practices such as the return to wearing a veil in countries like Egypt is used as a statement of ethnic identity (see Gadant, 1986).

In countries of immigration, these tendencies can cause inter-generational tensions, especially for girls who feel themselves trapped between two contradictory models of behaviour, and some-times oppressed by the domestic model. There is no question that girls defined as 'bad' can be subjected to very repressive treatment, as school and university counsellors well know. But the Greek-Australian secondary students whom I interviewed in 1980 also compared their own conditions relatively favourably with those of Anglo-Australian schoolfriends, mentioning the incidence of teenage pregnancies and rape as genuine hazards for girls whose families left them to their own devices (Bottomley, 1980, 1983). Maria Strintzos teases out some of the complexities of this situation and the way in which schools reinforce the 'ethnic equation' that, in her words, 'to be Greek is to be Good' (1984, p.35). But this kind of 'equation' is brought into question by comparisons with changes in Greece, as well as with the Australian environment.

In our study of 50 Greek households in the Sydney suburb of Marrickville in 1985–86, we also found that 78 per cent of respondents believed that their children had more freedom than they had had themselves, and everyone asserted that household decisions were mutual. However, in 98 per cent of households, the women had responsibility for housework, although they were also in paid employment in all but two cases. Most people knew of changes to the Family Law in Greece and only one expressed negative views on these changes. Everyone else described them as 'good', 'progressive', even 'great!'. More people criticised changes in Australia, but they tended to focus on sex education in schools. However, three young women argued that anti-discrimination and equal opportunity programs were 'ineffectual' and 'too weak' (Bottomley and Georgiou,

1988). Most respondents saw positive virtues in Greek families, despite a recognition that family closeness could also mean less freedom for young people and especially for girls. Our sample would have a built-in bias, however, in that those rejecting family life would hardly choose to live in a Greek household in Marrickville, which is a densely Greek suburb!

Another point of view about the agony (and some of the ecstasy) of family life is put by George Papaellinas in his book, *Ikons*, referred to earlier in chapters 4 and 8. His story, 'A Merchant's Widow', poignantly captures the suffering of an old woman, waiting in a darkened room for her grandson, who has rejected her. The old lady remembers her marriage, a husband who treated her with a respect that she has never discovered in 'the godless country' to which she emigrated, after his death. Now, having cherished her grandson as an heir to her husband's qualities, she finds herself an object of the boy's contempt – a contempt developed partly in the process of becoming 'Australian'.

And the boy would be cold and strange when she would come for him. She would have to search up and down the asphalt playground and she would find him and seize him by the arm and bend to kiss him and hug him and his smile would be as dry as the kiss he would plant on her cheek. And he walked slightly apart from her in her black, black clothes and the headscarf she wore like a shroud and she would have to prod him and push him and draw him back to her side. All around, the other children would giggle and she would dampen her expression and ask the boy about his day and he would grunt some reply and continue to pretend that he did not understand her language. He would grin a tentative smile back at the smirking children milling around them and he would shy away from her blackness and her pride would silence her and the next day she would wear the same clothes because this was a debt to the merchant. (Papaellinas, 1986, p.10)

As we saw in the last chapter, such insights into family life raise important questions about the constitution of subjectivities where people are, in several respects, 'from another place'.

To summarise briefly: 'migrant women' are frequently excluded from the leadership of ethnic organisations, and exploited as workers. They are also often exploited as unpaid labour in community welfare and in running community organisations. And, like many Anglo-Australian women, many of them are sexually oppressed at home and at work. For non-English-speaking women, this oppression can be compounded by problems of language and of the cultural expectations created by their own habitus and by those of members of the 'host' society. An example of this kind of compounding can be seen in a typical response to repetitive strain injuries which, as we have seen, are often incurred by migrant women workers. Michael Morrissey (1984) cites a case of a woman whose reported pains in her hand and wrist were treated as malingering – by her foreman, the nursing sister at the factory, and the insurance company's doctor – even though her own general practitioner had recommended surgery. Eventually, she was referred to a psychiatrist who told her that her problem was that she did not have a boyfriend and that she should go back to Greece if she was unhappy in Australia. Such hostility is regularly encountered by women such as this one, who was eventually treated by the Workers Health Centre. Another instance of the layering of structured unfreedom was in a large workplace in Sydney where a number of migrant workers were employed, and where some of the male employees set up a virtual prostitution racket by threatening women workers that they would 'tell their husbands' if they refused to co-operate. In other words, the husbands' expectations were themselves a source of oppression. These women would only talk anonymously by telephone, in their own languages, to women of the Ethnic Affairs Commission. Finally, the male 'organisers' lost their jobs.

Clearly, there is some resistance to oppression of this kind. Feminist initiatives have led to the establishment of anti-discrimination legislation and equal pay decisions, as well as women's health centres, child care centres, and women's refuges. The trade union movement has also established workers' health centres and centres for working women, and some unions are trying to do more for their migrant and female members. There are problems with most of these initiatives, as we have seen, and it is important to recognise the risk of imposing another form of assimilationism. For example, a recent 'Migrant Women's Speakout' insisted that a special refuge for non-English-speaking women be made a priority, arguing that migrant women would feel more comfortable with women who understood and could empathise with their circumstances. Most refuges are identified with radical feminism and are therefore unacceptable to a large number of migrants, male and female. Similarly, some ethno-specific child care centres and day care centres for the elderly have been established.

I believe that the most effective resistance to these structured unfreedoms can come from those who have experience of these three areas of definition and who can appreciate the interrelation between the three. But the tendency to marginalise one or more perspective is heightened in discussions that stress some essentialist 'us' versus 'them', thereby resorting to the very dichotomies that substitute categorising for thought and recreate distinctions that are usually based on claims to control of legitimate knowledge. The fragmenting possibilities of this kind of differentiation are kaleidoscopic. In most discourses about women and 'ethnics', the class perspective seems to cause most trouble, perhaps because the other two are, in the words of Anthias and Yuval-Davis, 'underpinned by a notion of a "natural" relation', whereas class is less easily reduced to an essence.

In a recent statement, women from the Italo-Australian workers organisation, FILEF, urged that feminists should examine the tendency to exclude young women, many working class women and 'those women who have chosen more traditional life styles', as well as women of non-English-speaking background (*Tribune*, October 21, 1987). Their own point of reference was probably the Italian women's movement, which, like the Greek organisations discussed in chapter 7, is linked to wider political views that encompass both class- and gender-based action. In Australia, action of this kind is much more marginal: this particular variant of political culture is not one that has been accepted under the rubric of multiculturalism.

CONNECTIONS

I have interwoven the three perspectives of class, gender and ethnicity throughout this discussion of experiences of work, health, and state intervention in the lives of non-English-speakers, and especially of Greek-Australians. At times, one or the other had priority, but I believe that one perspective without the others begs crucial questions. For example, in a thorough study of schools, families and social divisions, researchers found that they were unable to locate working class fathers who were 'just manual workers' and also Anglo-Australians. They tended to find foremen and leading hands; in the words of the political economists of migration, 'a labour aristocracy' (cf. Connell et al., 1982). As Collins (1984) and Lever Tracy have pointed out, the Australian working class is mostly non-Anglophone (Collins, 1988; Lever Tracy, 1985). But the implications of such statistical realities are virtually unexplored. Political economists refer to the ethnic segmentation of the workforce and the import of replaceable and potentially exploitable labour, but further analysis is minimal. We have no studies to compare with those of Hartz (1964), Gutman (1976), Kolko (1976) and Karabel (1979) which see migration as central to the history of the United States (see chapter 2).

Furthermore, as I have argued all through this book, the assumption that culture is co-terminous with ethnicity can prevent commentators from examining the processes by which people are incorporated, subjected or mobilised to resist. Ethnicists, for example, emphasise a kind of a historical and a political culturalism, while political economists tend to deduce action and interactions from structures, under-estimating the significance of pre-migration experience and continuing contact with, and understanding of the world beyond Australia.

Nevertheless, some highly sophisticated work has been done in Australia that does take account of the three dimensions discussed here, as well as the politics of culture in several spheres of activity, including work (Lever Tracy, 1984); families (de Lepervanche, 1990); religion (Humphrey,1984a, b); community organisations (Kakakios and van der Velden, 1984; Turpin 1990); language (Kalantzis et al., 1990); education (Foster, 1989); multicultural policy (Jayasuriya, 1990) and, more generally, Australian nationalism (Castles et al., 1988; Kapferer, 1988; de Lepervanche, 1990).

The bicentennial celebration of 1988 was itself a powerful statement about control of symbolic capital, the 'natural right' to represent the Australian nation. It is significant that this date was chosen rather than the centenary of federation, which might have been a genuine 'celebration of a nation', rather than what was basically the establishment of an English prison colony. Benedict Anderson has demonstrated that the construction of imagined communities is based on a concept of deep, horizontal comradeship that disregards inequality, exploitation and difference (1983). But, as we have seen, despite the powerful role of the state, there is always conflict over the power to make groups, to represent social divisions, to define traditions and doxa. In this process, the work of intellectuals is central, although we need to be aware of the extent to which some of our work is already written and our understandings pre-formed. As Italo Calvino implied, 'in any book there is a part that is the author's and a part that is a collective and anonymous work' (1982, p.99 quoted in chapter 1 above). Perhaps the most we can do is to remain sceptical of available representations, while continuing to ask questions about what, and who, is *not* being represented.

Throughout this book I have been concerned with these questions and with the use of such concepts as tradition and ethnicity that can both reflect and obscure forms of domination. I have also suggested ways of seeing and hearing practices such as dance and music, and giving closer attention to literature, as instruments of understanding. Finally, I have developed international and anthropological perspectives that allow for both comparisons and specificities.

Bibliography

ACPEA (Australian Council on Population and Ethnic Affairs) (1982) *Multiculturalism for all Australians* (Canberra: Australian Government Printer)

AEAC (Australian Ethnic Affairs Council) (1977) *Australia as a multicultural society* (Canberra: Australian Government Printer)

AIMA (Australian Institute for Multicultural Affairs) (1985) *Ageing in a multicultural society* (Melbourne: Australian Government Printer)

Allen, P. (1979) 'Internal migration and changing dowry in modern Greece' in Koumoulides, J. T. A. (ed.) *Greece: past and present* (Muncie, Indiana: Ball State University Press)

Anderson, B. (1983) *Imagined communities* (London: Verso)

Anthias, Floya (1983) 'Sexual divisions and ethnic adaptation: the case of Greek-Cypriot women' in Phizacklea, A. (ed.) *One way ticket: migration and female labour* (London: Routledge and Kegan Paul) pp.73–94

Anthias, Floya and Yuval-Davis, Nira (1983) 'Contextualising feminism – gender, ethnic and class divisions', *Feminist Review*, No. 15, November, pp.62–75

Ardener, S. (ed.) (1975) *Perceiving women* (London: Malaby Press)

Ariès, P. (1973) *Centuries of Childhood* (Harmondsworth: Penguin)

Asante, M. K. (1989) *The Afrocentric idea* (Philadelphia: Temple University Press)

Attali, J. (1977) *Bruits: essais sur l'économie politique de la musique* (Paris: Presses Universitaires de France)

——(1985) tr. Brian Massumi, *Noise: the political economy of music*, (Minneapolis: University of Minnesota Press)

Bachofen, J. (1967) tr. Ralph Manheim, *Myth, religion and mother right* (London: Routledge and Kegan Paul)

Barker, Martin (1981) *The new racism* (London: Junction Books)

Barrett, M. and McIntosh, M. (1982) *The anti-social family* (London: Verso)

——(1985) 'Ethnocentrism and socialist feminist theory', *Feminist Studies*, No. 20, Summer, pp.23–47

Barthes, R. (1985) tr. Richard Howard, 'The Greek theatre' in Barthes, R. *The responsibility of forms* (New York: Hill and Wang)

Bell, Daniel (1975) 'Ethnicity and social change' in Glazer, N. and Moynihan, D. (eds) *Ethnicity: theory and experience* (Cambridge: Harvard University Press)

Bellow, S. (1971) *Mr Sammler's planet* (Harmondsworth: Penguin)

Berger, J. (1968) *Working class suburb: a study of auto workers in suburbia* (Berkeley: University of California Press)

——(1972) *Ways of seeing* (London: Writers and Readers Publishing Co-operative)

——(with Jean Mohr) (1975) *A seventh man* (London: Penguin)

Bien, Peter (1987) Review of George Kanarakis' *The literary presence of Greeks in Australia, Journal of Modern Greek Studies*, Vol. 5, No. 1, May, pp.120-3

Birnbaum, N. (1971) *Towards a critical sociology* (New York: Oxford University Press)

Blauner, B. (1989) *Black lives: white lives. Three decades of race relations in America* (Berkeley: University of California Press)

Bottomley, G. (1968) 'Indonesian millenialism in comparative perspective', unpublished BA (hons) thesis, Dept of Anthropology, University of Sydney

——(1974) 'Some Greek sex roles: ideals, expectations and action in Australia and Greece', *Australian and New Zealand Journal of Sociology*, Vol. 10, No. 1, February, 1974, pp.8-16

——(1975) 'Migrant women' in Mercer, J. (ed.) *The other half* (Melbourne: Penguin)

——(1979) *After the Odyssey: a study of Greek Australians* (Brisbane: University of Queensland Press)

——(1980) 'Eurydice in the underworld: Mediterranean women in Australia', *Refractory Girl*, Nos 20-21, October, pp.48-52

——(1981) 'Migration studies: Quo vademus? (Quid facemus?)', *Australia and New Zealand Journal of Sociology*, Vol. 17, No. 3, November, pp.70-4

——(1983) (co-ed. with Burns, A. and Jools, P.) *Family in the Modern World* (Sydney: Allen and Unwin)

——(1984a) 'Women on the move: migration and feminism' in Bottomley, G. and de Lepervanche, M. (eds) *Ethnicity, Class and Gender in Australia* (Sydney: Allen and Unwin), pp.98-108

——(1984b) *The export of people: emigration from and return migration to Greece* (Wollongong: Centre for Multicultural Studies)

——(1984c) 'Mediterranean women in Australia: an overview' (paper presented to a conference of Mediterranean Women's Organisations, Delphi, Greece), published as Multicultural Australia Paper No. 35 (Clearing House on Migration Issues, Melbourne)

——(1985) 'Perpetuation de la dot chez les Grecs d'Australie: transformation et ré-négociation des pratiques traditionnelles' in Piault, C. (ed.) *Familles et biens en Grèce et à Chypre* (L'Harmattan, Paris), pp.145-64

——(1987) 'Cultures, multiculturalism and the politics of representation', *Journal of Intercultural Studies* 8, 2, pp.1-9

——(1988) 'Ethnicity, race and nationalism in Australia: some critical perspectives', *Australian Journal of Social Issues* 23, 3, pp.169-83

——(1991) 'Representing the second generation: Subjects, objects and ways of knowing' in Bottomley, de Lepervanche and Martin (eds) *Intersexions: gender/class/culture/ethnicity* (Sydney: Allen and Unwin) pp.92-109

Bottomley, G. and de Lepervanche, M. (eds) (1984) *Ethnicity, class and gender in Australia* (Sydney: Allen and Unwin)

Bottomley, G., de Lepervanche, M. and Martin, J. (eds) (1991) *Inter-sexions: gender/class/culture/ethnicity* (Sydney: Allen and Unwin)

Bottomley, G. and Georgiou, V. (1988) 'Multiculturalism in practice: a study of Greek Australian families in Sydney' in Tamis, A. and Kapardis, G. (eds) *Greeks in Australia* (Melbourne: River Seine Publications)

Bottomley, G. and Lechte, J. (1990) 'Nation and diversity in France', *Journal of Intercultural Studies* 11, 1, pp.49-72

Bottomley, G. and Raftis, A. (1984) 'Ritual dance and communal celebrations in rural Greece', *Journal of Intercultural Studies*, Vol. 5, No. 1, pp.22-32

Bourdieu, P. (1977) tr. Richard Nice, *Outline of a theory of practice* (Cambridge: Cambridge University Press)

——(1980) *Questions de sociologie* (Paris: Les Editions de Minuit)

——(1986) tr. Richard Nice, *Distinction: a social critique of the judgement of taste* (London: Routledge and Kegan Paul)

——(1987) *Choses dites* (Paris: Editions de Minuit)

——(1990) tr. M. Adamson, *In other words: essays towards a reflexive sociology* (Cambridge, U.K.: Polity Press)

Brett, Judith (1983) 'On clowns and migrant artists', *Meanjin*, Vol. 42, No. 1, March, pp.140-1

Calvino, Italo (1982) *The uses of literature* (San Diego: Harcourt Brace Jovanovich)

Campbell, J. (1964) *Honour, family and patronage* (Oxford: Oxford University Press)

——(1976) 'Regionalism and local community' in Dimen, M. and Friedl, E. (eds) *Regional variation in modern Greece and Cyprus: towards a perspective on the ethnography of Greece. Annals of the N.Y. Academy of Sciences*, Vol. 268, pp.18-27

Cappiello, Rosa (1981) *Paese fortunato* (Rome: Feltrinelli)

Caraveli, Anna (1986) 'The Bitter Wounding: The Lament as Social Protest in Rural Greece' in Dubisch, J. (ed.) *Gender and power in rural Greece* (Princeton, N.J.: Princeton University Press)

Carby, H. (1982) 'White woman listen! Black feminism and the boundaries of sisterhood' in Centre for Contemporary Cultural Studies, *The empire strikes back* (London: Hutchinson)

Castan, C. (1990) *Dimitris Tsaloumas: poet* (Melbourne: Elikia Books Publications)

Castles, S. and Kosack, G. (1973) *Immigrant workers and class structure in western Europe* (London: Oxford University Press for the Institute of Race Relations)

Castles, S. with H. Booth and T. Wallace (1986) *Here for good: western Europe's new ethnic minorities* (London: Pluto Press)

Castles, S., Kalantzis, M., Cope, B. and Morrissey, M. (1988) *Mistaken identity: multiculturalism and the demise of nationalism in Australia* (Sydney: Pluto Press)

Cavounidis, Jennifer (1983) 'Capitalist development and women's work in Greece', *Journal of Modern Greek Studies*, Vol. 1, No. 2, pp.321–38

Centre for Contemporary Cultural Studies (1982) *The empire strikes back* (London: Hutchinson)

Centre for Working Women (1986) *Women outworkers* (Melbourne: Centre for Working Women Co-operative Ltd)

Clifford, J. and Marcus, G. (eds) (1986) *Writing culture: the poetics and politics of ethnography* (Berkeley: University of California Press)

Clifford, J. (1988) *The predicament of culture* (Cambridge, Mass.: Harvard University Press)

Code civil hellénique (1956) (Tr. de l'Institut Hellénique de Droit International et Etranger)

Collins, J. (1988) *Migrant hands in a distant land* (Sydney: Pluto Press)

Connell, R. W. (1987) *Gender and power* (Sydney: Allen and Unwin)

Connell, R. W., Ashenden, D. J., Kessler, S., Dowsett, G. (eds) (1982) *Making the difference: schools, families and social division* (Sydney: Allen and Unwin)

Constantinides, E. (1983) 'Andreiomeni: The female warrior in Greek folk songs', *Journal of Modern Greek Studies*, Vol. 1, No. 1, May, pp.63–72

Cowan, J. (1990) *Dance and the body politic in northern Greece* (Princeton, N.J.: Princeton University Press)

Cox, O. C. (1948) *Caste, class and race* (New York: Doubleday)

CRASTE (Committee to Review Australian Studies in Tertiary Education) (1987) *Windows onto worlds* (Canberra: Australian Government Printer)

Curthoys, A. and Markus, A. (eds) (1978) *Who are our enemies? Racism and the working class in Australia* (Sydney: Hale and Iremonger)

Damianakos, S. (1977) *I Koinonioloyia tou rembetikou* (The sociology of the *rembetiko*) (Athens, Ermeias. In Greek)

Davis, E. G. (1972) *The first sex* (Baltimore, Md: Penguin)

De Beauvoir, S. ((1949) 1972) *The second sex*, tr. and ed. H. M. Parshley (Harmondsworth: Penguin)

——(1977) *Old age* (Harmondsworth: Penguin)

De Lepervanche, M. (1980) 'From race to ethnicity', *The Australian and New Zealand Journal of Sociology*, Vol. 16, No. 1, March, pp.24–37

——(1984a) *Indians in a white Australia* (Sydney: Allen and Unwin)

——(1984b) 'The naturalness of inequality' in Bottomley, G. and de Lepervanche, M. (eds) *Ethnicity, class and gender in Australia* (Sydney: Allen and Unwin)

——(1984c) 'Immigrants and ethnic groups' in Encel, S. and Bryson, L. (eds) *Australian society: introductory essays* (4th edn) (Melbourne: Longman Cheshire)

——(1990) 'Holding it all together: multiculturalism, nationalism, women and the state in Australia' (paper presented at the XIIth World Congress of Sociology, Madrid)

De Lepervanche, M. and Bottomley, G. (eds) *The cultural construction of race* (Sydney: Studies in Society and Culture)

Delaruelle, J. (1990) 'Migratory birds – wandering thoughts', *Island*, 42, Autumn, pp.67–71

Dell'Oso, A. M. (1987) 'Scaling the linguistic wall of indifference' in Gunew, S. (ed.) *Displacements* (Geelong: Deakin University Press)

DIEA (Department of Immigration and Ethnic Affairs) (1981) *Profile 81: 1981 census data on persons born in Greece* (Canberra: Australian Government Printer)

Dimen, M. and Friedl, E. (1976) *Regional variations in modern Greece and Cyprus* (New York: Academy of Sciences)

Dimen, M. (1983) 'Servants and sentries – women, power and social reproduction in Kriovrisi', *Journal of Modern Greek Studies*, Vol. 1, No. 1, pp.225–42

Donzelot, J. (1979) *The policing of families* (New York: Pantheon)

Doumanis, Mariella (1983) *Mothering in Greece: from collectivism to individualism* (London: Academic Press)

Dritsas, M. (1981) 'Changes in the character of the Greek Parliament', *Greek Review of Social Research*, No. 41, January–April, pp.2–5

Dubisch, J. (1983) 'Greek women: sacred or profane', *Journal of Modern Greek Studies*, I (1), pp.195–202

——(ed.) (1986) *Gender and power in rural Greece* (Princeton, N.J.: Princeton University Press)

Du Boulay, J. (1974) *Portrait of a Greek mountain village* (Oxford: Clarendon Press)

——(1982) 'The Greek vampire: a study of cyclic symbolism in marriage and death', *Man*, No. 2, June, pp.219–35

——(1986) 'Women – images of their nature and destiny in rural Greece', in Dubisch, J. (ed.) *Gender and Power in rural Greece* (Princeton, N.J.: Princeton University Press)

Dyer, Geoff (1986) *Ways of telling: the work of John Berger* (London: Pluto Press)

Encel, S. (ed.) (1981) *The ethnic dimension: papers on ethnicity and pluralism by Jean Martin* (Sydney: Allen and Unwin)

Engels, F. ((1844) 1970) *The origin of the family, private property and the state*, in *Marx and Engels Selected Works*, Vol. 3 (Moscow: Progress Publishers)

Erikson, E. (1968) *Identity: youth and crisis* (London: Faber)

Fabian, J. (1983) *Time and the other: how anthropology makes its object* (New York: Columbia University Press)

Fischer, M. J. (1986) 'Ethnicity and post-modern arts of memory' in Clifford, J. and Marcus, G. E. (eds) *Writing culture: the poetics and politics of ethnography* (Berkeley: University of California Press)

Foster, L. (1988) *Diversity and multicultural education* (Sydney: Allen and Unwin)

Foucault, M. (1982) 'The subject and power', Afterword in Dreyfus, H. and Rabinow, P. (eds) *Michel Foucault: beyond structuralism and hermeneutics* (Chicago: Harvester Press)

Frazer, J. G. (1976 edn) *The golden bough: a study in magic and religion* (London: Macmillan)

Frazier, E. F. (1947) 'Sociological theory and race relations', *American Sociological Review*, Vol. 12, June, pp.265–71

Friedl, E. (1962) *Vasilika: a village in modern Greece* (New York: Holt Rinehart Winston)

——(1967) 'The position of women: appearance and reality', *Anthropological Quarterly*, 40, 3, pp.97–108

——(1976) 'Kinship, class and selective migration' in Peristiany, J. G. (ed.) *Mediterranean family structures* (Cambridge: Cambridge University Press)

Gadant, M. (ed.) (1986) tr. A. M. Berrett, *Women of the Mediterranean* (London: Zed books)

Gans, H. (1962) *The urban villagers* (New York: The Free Press)

Geertz, C. (1973) *The interpretation of cultures* (New York: Basic Books)

Giannaris, G. (1973) *Mikis Theodorakis: music and social change* (London: George Allen and Unwin)

Giddens, A. (1987) *Social theory and modern sociology* (Cambridge: Polity Press)

Giles, Z. (1989) *Miracle of the waters* (Melbourne: Penguin Books)

Gilroy, P. (1987) *There ain't no black in the union jack* (London: Hutchinson)

——(1988/89) 'Cruciality and the frog's perspective', *Third Text* 5, Winter, pp.33–44

Glazer, N. and Moynihan, D. (1964) *Beyond the melting pot* (Cambridge, Mass.: Massachusetts Institute of Technology Press)

Glazer, N. and Moynihan, D. (eds) (1975) *Ethnicity: theory and experience* (Cambridge and London: Harvard University Press)

Goody, J. and Tambiah, S. J. (1973) *Bridewealth and dowry* (Cambridge: Cambridge University Press)

Gordon, M. (1964) *Assimilation in American life* (New York: Oxford University Press)

Gorecki, Vanda Moraes (1987) *Family migration and S. American women in Australia*, unpublished PhD thesis, Department of Anthropology, University of Sydney

Gouldner, A. (1971) *The coming crisis of western sociology* (London: Heinemann)

Graves, Robert (1961) *The white goddess* (London: Faber)

Grundy, Philip (1983) Translator's introduction to Tsaloumas, D. *The observatory* (Brisbane: University of Queensland Press)

Guilcher, J. M. (1969) *La contredanse et les renouvellements de la danse française* (Paris: Mouton)

Gunew, S. (1983) 'Migrant women writers: who's on whose margins?', *Meanjin*, Vol. 42, No. 1, March, pp.16-25

Gutman, Herbert (1976) *Work, culture and society in industrialising America* (New York: Knopf)

Hacker, A. (1988) 'Black crime, white racism', *New York Review of Books*, March 3, pp.36-41

Hall, Stuart (1980) 'Race, articulation and societies structured in dominance', *UNESCO: sociological theories: race and colonialism* (Paris: Mouton)

——(1981) 'Cultural studies: two paradigms' in Bennett, T., Martin, G., Mercer, C., Woollacott, J. (eds) *Culture, ideology and social process: a reader* (Milton Keynes: Open University Press), pp.19-37

——(1987) 'Minimal selves' in *Identity: the real me* (ICA Documents No. 6, London, Institute of Contemporary Arts), pp.44-6

Hall, S. et al. (1978) *Policing the crisis: mugging, the state, and law and order* (London: Macmillan)

Handler, R. (1988) *Nationalism and the politics of culture in Quebec* (Madison: University of Wisconsin Press)

Harichaux, P., Rougier, C. and Palis, M. (1982) *Activités physiques et troisième âge* (Paris: Chiron Sports)

Hartz, L. (1964) *The founding of new societies* (New York: Harcourt Brace Jovanovich)

Harvey, D. (1989) *The condition of postmodernity* (Oxford: Basil Blackwell)

Herskovits, Melville (1958) *The myth of the Negro past* (Boston: Beacon Press)

Herzfeld, M. (1982) *Ours once more: folklore, ideology and the making of modern Greece* (Austin: University of Texas Press)

——(1983) 'Semantic slippage and moral fall: the rhetoric of chastity in rural Greek society', *Journal of Modern Greek Studies*, No. 1, pp.161-72

——(1985) *The poetics of manhood* (Princeton, N.J.: Princeton University Press)

——(1986) 'Within and without: the category of 'female' in the ethnography of modern Greece' in Dubisch, J. (ed.) *Gender and Power in Rural Greece* (Princeton, N.J.: Princeton University Press)

——(1987) *Anthropology through the looking glass* (Cambridge: Cambridge University Press)

Hirschon, R. (1983) 'Women, the aged and religious activity: oppositions and complementarity in an urban locality', *Journal of Modern Greek Studies*, Vol. 1, 1, May, pp.113-29

Holst, G. (1975) *Road to Rembetika* (Athens: Anglo-Hellenic Publishing)

Howe, I. (1986) *Socialism and America* (New York: Harcourt Brace Jovanovich)

Huber, R. (1977) *From pasta to pavlova* (Brisbane: University of Queensland Press)

Humphrey, M. (1984) 'Religion, law and family disputes in a Lebanese Muslim community in Sydney' in Bottomley, G. and de Lepervanche, M. (eds) *Ethnicity, class and gender in Australia* (Sydney: Allen and Unwin)

Jakubowicz, A. (1981) 'State and ethnicity: multiculturalism as ideology', *Australia and New Zealand Journal of Sociology*, Vol. 17, No. 3, pp.4–13

——(1983) 'Equality and the objective' in *The Socialist objective: labor and socialism* (Sydney: Hale and Iremonger)

——(1984) 'Ethnicity, multiculturalism and neo-conservatism' in Bottomley, G. and de Lepervanche, M. (eds) *Ethnicity, class and gender in Australia* (Sydney: Allen and Unwin)

Jakubowicz, A., Morrissey, M. and Palser, J. (1984) *Ethnicity, class and social policy in Australia* (SWRC Reports and Proceedings, No. 46) (Sydney: Social Welfare Research Centre)

Jayasuriya, L. (1990) 'Rethinking Australian multiculturalism: towards a new paradigm', *Australian Quarterly*, Autumn, Vol. 62, No. 1

Jayawardena, C. (1963) *Conflict and solidarity in a Guyanese Plantation* (London: Athlone Press)

——(1968) 'Migration and social change', *Geographical Review*, No. 58, pp.426–49

——(1978) Lectures 'Sociology of Migration' course, Macquarie University, Sydney

——(1980) 'Culture and ethnicity in Guyana and Fiji', *Man*, 15, pp.430–50

Johnson, R. (1986) 'The story so far: and further transformations?' in Punter, D. (ed.) *Introduction to contemporary cultural studies* (London and New York: Longman)

Jupp, J. (ed.) (1984) *Ethnic politics in Australia* (Sydney: Allen and Unwin)

Kakakios, M. and van der Velden, J. (1984) 'Migrant communities and class politics: the Greek community in Australia' in Bottomley, G. and de Lepervanche, M. (eds) *Ethnicity, class and gender in Australia* (Sydney: Allen and Unwin)

Kaklamanakis, K. (1972) *The position of the Greek woman in family, community and polity* (Athens: Paidhia, in Greek)

Kalamaras, V. (1956) *The bread trap/Mia faka me Psomaki* (bilingual edition) tr. Vasso Kalamaras, Reg Durack and June Kingdon (Melbourne: Elikia Books)

Kanarakis, G. (1985) *I logotechniki parousia ton Ellinon stin Australia* (*The literary presence of Greeks in Australia*) (Athens: Idrima Neollinikon Spudon)

——(1987) *Greek voices in Australia: a tradition of prose, poetry and drama* (Sydney: Pergamon Press, ANU)

Kapferer, B. (1988) *Legends of people: myths of state* (Washington and London: Smithsonian Institute Press)

Karabel, Jerome (1979) 'The failure of American socialism reconsidered', *Socialist Register*, pp.204–27

Kazantzakis, Nikos (1959) *The Odyssey: a modern sequel* tr. Kimon Friar (London: Secker and Warburg)

——(1961) *Zorba the Greek* (London: Faber and Faber)

Kilpatrick, D. B. (1980) *Function and style in Pontic dance music* (Athens: Committee of Pontic Studies)

Kingston, M. H. (1976) *The woman warrior* (London: Picador)

——(1980) *China men* (London: Picador)

Kolko, Gabriel (1976) *Main currents in modern American history* (New York: Harper and Row)

Krili-Kevans, Yiota (1984) *Konda sti glossa* (Sydney: Inner City Education Centre)

Kristeva, Julia (1986) 'The system and the speaking subject' in Moi, T. (ed.) *The Kristeva reader* (Oxford: Basil Blackwell)

——(1988) *Etrangers à nous-mêmes* (Paris: Fayard)

Lambiri-Dimaki, I. (1972) 'Dowry in modern Greece: an institution on the cross roads between persistence and decline' in Safilios-Rothschild, C. (ed.) *Toward a sociology of women* (Lexington, Mass.: Xerox), pp.73–81

Lasch, C. (1979) *Haven in a heartless world: the family besieged* (New York: Basic Books)

Lees, S. (1986) 'Sex, race and culture; feminism and the limits of cultural pluralism', *Feminist Review*, 22, Spring, pp.92–102

Lever, Tracy C. (1985) 'The segmentation and articulation of the working class: an exploration of the impact of postwar Australian immigration' (unpublished PhD thesis, Flinders University, Adelaide, South Australia)

Lever, Tracy C. and Quinlan, M. (1988) *A divided working class* (Routledge and Kegan Paul)

Lévi-Strauss, C. (1985) *The view from afar* (New York: Basic Books)

Lewin, K. (1952) *Field theory in social science* (London: Tavistock)

Lipsitz, G. (1990) *Time passages: collective memory and American popular culture* (Minneapolis: University of Minnesota Press)

Lloyd, Genevieve (1984) *The man of reason: 'male' and 'female' in western philosophy* (London: Methuen)

Loukakis, A. (1981) *For the patriarch* (Brisbane: University of Queensland Press)

Lyotard, J. F. (1984) *The postmodern condition: a report on knowledge* (Minneapolis: University of Minnesota Press)

Mandel, R. (1983) 'Sacrifice at the bridge of Arta: sex role and the manipulation of power', *Journal of Modern Greek Studies*, Vol. 1, No. 1, May, 1983, pp.173–84

Markus, A. and Ricklefs, (eds) (1985) *Surrender Australia?* (Sydney: Allen and Unwin)

Marre, J. and Charlton, H. (1985) *Beats of the heart: popular music of the world* (London: Pluto Press)

Martin, J. (1965) *Refugee settlers: a study of displaced persons in Australia* (Canberra: Australian National University Press)

——(1967) 'Extended kinship ties: an Adelaide study', *Australia and New Zealand Journal of Sociology*, 3, 1, pp.44–63

——(1970) 'Suburbia: community and network' in Davies, A. and Encel, S. (eds) *Australian society: a sociological introduction* 2nd edn (Melbourne: Cheshire)

——(1975) 'Family and bureaucracy' in Price, C. (ed.) *Greeks in Australia* (Canberra: ANU Press)

——(1978) *The migrant presence* (Sydney: Allen and Unwin)

Martin, Jeannie (1983) 'The development of multiculturalism' in Cass, M. (chairman) *Report to the Minister for Immigration and Ethnic Affairs*, Vol. 2 (Canberra: Australian Government Printer)

——(1984) 'Non-English-speaking women' in Bottomley G. and de Lepervanche, M. (eds) (q.v.)

——(1986) 'Non English speaking women in Australia', in Grieve, N. and Burns, A. (eds) *Australian women: new feminist perspectives*, pp.233–47

Matthews, S. (1979) *The social world of old women* (London: Sage)

Mayer, Adrian (1961) *Peasants in the pacific* (London: Routledge and Kegan Paul)

McCallum, J. (1990) 'The mosaic of ethnicity and health in later life' in Reid, J. and Trompf, P. (eds) *The health of immigrant Australia* (Sydney: Harcourt Brace Jovanovich)

McCaughey, D. (1988) *Piecing together a shared vision* (Sydney: Australian Broadcasting Corporation)

McNeill, W. H. (1978) *The metamorphosis of Greece since World War II* (Oxford: Basil Blackwell)

Mercer, J. (ed.) (1975) *The other half* (Melbourne: Penguin)

Miles, R. (1982) *Racism and migrant labour* (London: Routledge and Kegan Paul)

——(1988) 'Beyond the race concept: the reproduction of racism in England' in de Lepervanche, M. and Bottomley, G. (eds) (q.v.)

——(1989) *Racism* (London: Routledge and Kegan Paul)

Mills, C. W. (1950) *The Puerto Rican journey: New York's newest migrants* (with C. Senior and R. K. Goldsen) (New York: Oxford University Press)

——(1959) *The sociological imagination* (New York: Oxford University Press)

Mitchell, Juliet (1971) *Woman's estate* (Harmondsworth: Penguin Books)

Morin, E. (1989) 'L'Europe est trop blanche,' entretien dans *L'Europe multiraciale* (Paris: Documents Observateur), pp.182–6

Morrissey, M. (1984) 'Migrantness, culture and ideology' in Bottomley, G. and de Lepervanche, M. (eds) (q.v.)

Morokvasic, M. (1983) 'Women in migration: beyond the reductionist outlook' in Phizacklea, A. (ed.) (q.v.)

Mouzelis, Nicos (1978) *Modern Greece: facets of underdevelopment* (London: Macmillan)

Myrdal, G. (1972 edn) *An American dilemma: the Negro problem and modern democracy*, Vols I and II (New York: Pantheon)

Nabokov, V. (1960) *Pnin* (Harmondsworth: Penguin)

Naipaul, V. S. (1970) *An area of darkness* (London: Penguin)

Newman, W. M. (1973) *American pluralism* (New York: Harper and Rowe)

Nikolaidou, M. (1979) *The Greek woman today: work and struggle* (Athens: Kastaniotis, in Greek)

Nygh, P. L. (1981) *Guide to the Family Law Act, 1975* (Sydney: Butterworth)

Paine, S. (1974) *Exporting workers: the Turkish case* (Cambridge: Cambridge University Press)

Papaellinas, George (1986) *Ikons* (Australia: Penguin Books)

Papastergiadis, Nikos (1985) 'The ideological practice of multiculturalism', *Chroniko*

——(1986) 'A crack in the column 1: the new language', *Arena*, 74, p.137

Park, R. and Burgess, E. (1921) *Introduction to the science of sociology* (Chicago: University of Chicago Press)

Parkhill, Peter (1983) 'Two folk epics from Melbourne', *Meanjin*, Vol. 42, No. 1, March, 1983, pp.120–39

Parmar, P. (1982) 'Gender, race and class: Asian women in resistance' in Centre for Contemporary Cultural Studies, *The empire strikes back* (London: Hutchinson)

——(1989) 'Other kinds of dreams', *Feminist Review*, 31, Spring, pp.55–65

Parsons, T. (1951) *The social system* (Glencoe: The Free Press)

Pateman, C. and Gross, E. (eds) (1986) *Feminist challenges: social and political theory* (Sydney: Allen and Unwin)

Patterson, S. (1963) *Dark strangers* (London: Tavistock)

Peristiany, J. G. (1976) 'Introduction' in Peristiany, J. G. (ed.) *Mediterranean family structures* (Cambridge: Cambridge University Press), pp.1–26

Petrides, T. (1975) *Greek dances* (Athens: Lycabettus Press)

Pettman, J. (1988) 'Whose country is it anyway? Cultural politics, racism and the construction of being Australian', *Journal of Intercultural Studies*, 9, 1, pp.1–24

Phizacklea, A. (ed.) (1983) *One way ticket: migration and female labour* (London: Routledge and Kegan Paul)

Piault, C. (ed.) (1985) *Familles et biens en Grèce et à Chypre* (Paris: L'Harmattan)

Piore, M. (1979) *Birds of passage* (Cambridge: Cambridge University Press)

II.O. (1989) *Fitzroy poems* (Fitzroy, Melbourne: Collective Effort Press)

Powles, J. and Gifford, S. (1990) 'How healthy are Australia's immigrants?' in Reid, J. and Trompf, P. (eds) *The health of immigrant Australia* (Sydney: Harcourt Brace Jovanovich)

Price, C. (1987) *Ethnic groups in Australia* (Canberra: Australian Immigration Research Centre)

Psacharopoulos, G. (1983) 'Sex Discrimination in the Greek Labour Market' in *Journal of Modern Greek Studies*, Vol. 1, No. 2, October, pp.339-72

Rabinow, Paul (1986) 'Representations are social facts: modernity and post-modernity in anthropology' in Clifford, J. and Marcus, G. (eds) *Writing culture: the poetics and politics of ethnography* (Berkeley: University of California Press)

Raftis, A. (1983) 'La place du corps dans la formation en expression-communication' (paper presented to the 6th meeting of the Association des Formateurs en Expression–Communication, Grenoble, France)

——(1986) *O Kosmos tou Ellinikou Horou (The world of Greek dance)* (Athens: Polytypo, in Greek)

——(1987) *The world of Greek dance* (Athens: Finedawn Publishers)

Ramazanoglu, C. (1989) *Feminism and the contradictions of oppression* (London: Routledge and Kegan Paul)

Rex, J. and Tomlinson, S. (1979) *Colonial immigrants in a British city* (London: Routledge and Kegan Paul)

Rex, J. (1986) *Race and ethnicity* (Milton Keynes: Open University Press)

Rosaldo, M. (1983) 'Moral/analytic dilemmas posed by the intersection of feminism and social science' in Horan, N. et al. (eds) *Social science as moral inquiry* (New York: Columbia University Press)

Roussou, M. (1985) 'Systeme dotal et identité feminine dans la campagne chypriote' in Piault, C. (ed.) (q.v.)

Rushdie, S. (with Gunter Grass) (1987) 'Writing for a future' in Bourne, B., Eichler, U. and Herman, D. (eds) *Writers and politics*, from the Channel 4 television series *Voices* (Nottingham: Spokesman Hobo Press)

Russell, C. (1981) *The ageing experience* (Sydney: Allen and Unwin)

Rust, F. (1969) *Dance in society* (London: Routledge and Kegan Paul)

Said, Edward (1978) *Orientalism* (Harmondsworth: Penguin Books)

——(1985) 'Orientalism Reconsidered' in *Race and Class*, xxvii, 2, pp.1-15

Salamone, S. D. and Stanton, J. B. (1986) in Dubisch, J. (ed.) *Gender and power in rural Greece* (Princeton, N.J.: Princeton University Press)

Saliou, Monique (1986) 'The processes of women's subordination in primitive and archaic Greece' in Coontz, S. and Henderson, P. (eds) *Women's work, men's property: The origins of gender and class* (London: Verso)

Sant Cassia, P. (1985) 'Politiques matrimoniales. Usages stratégiques de la dot dans un village chypriote grec' in Piault, C. (ed.) (q.v.)

SBS (Special Broadcasting Service, Sydney) (1988) *Witch hunt*, semidocumentary film

Schneider, J. and Schneider, P. (1977) *Culture and political economy in western Sicily* (New York: Academic Press)

Schutz, A. (1964) 'The stranger' in Brodersen, A. (ed.) *Collected papers of Alfred Schutz* (The Hague: Martinus Nijhoff)

Segalen, M. (ed.) (1989) *L'autre et le semblable* (Paris: Presses du CNRS)

Sennett, R. and Cobb, J. (1971) *The hidden injuries of class* (Cambridge: Cambridge University Press)

Sgro, S., Pieri, S. and Risk, M. (1980) 'Italian migrant women: participation in the women's movement', paper presented at the 2nd Women and Labour Conference, Melbourne

Shapiro, R. (1985) 'Echange matrimonial et travail féminin. Les paradoxes de la modernité' in Piault, C. (ed.) (q.v.)

Sluga, Glenda (1987) 'The migrant dreaming', *Journal of Intercultural Studies*, Vol. 8, No. 2, pp.40-9

Smith, A. (1981) *The ethnic revival* (Cambridge: Cambridge University Press)

Smolicz, J. (1981) 'Core values and cultural identity', *Ethnic and Racial Studies*, IV, pp.75-90

Sontag, S. (1978) *Illness as Metaphor* (New York: Farrar, Strows and Giroux)

Spencer, P. (ed.) (1985) *Society and the dance: the social anthropology of process and performance* (Cambridge: Cambridge University Press)

Stamiris, Eleni (1986) 'The women's movement in Greece', *New Left Review*, No. 158, pp.98-112

Steinberg, S. (1981) *The ethnic myth: race, ethnicity and class in America* (Boston: Beacon Press)

Storer, D. (ed.) (1976) '. . . But I wouldn't want my wife to work here . . .' (Melbourne: Centre for Urban Research and Action)

Strathern, Marilyn (1985) 'Dislodging a world view: challenge and counter-challenge in the relationship between feminism and anthropology', *Australian Feminist Studies*, No. 1, pp.1-25

Strintzos, Maria (1984) 'To be Greek is to be good', *Cultural Politics*, Melbourne Working Papers, Series 5 (Melbourne: Department of Education, University of Melbourne)

Sutton, Susan B. (1986) 'Family and work: new patterns for village women in Athens', *Journal of Modern Greek Studies*, Vol. 4, No. 1, May, pp.33-49

Tait, D. and Gibson, K. (1987) 'Economic and ethnic restructuring: an analysis of migrant labour in Sydney', *Journal of Intercultural Studies*, Vol. 8, No. 1, pp.1-26

Taylor, C. (1989) *Sources of the self: the making of the modern identity* (Cambridge, Mass.: Harvard University Press)

Thomas, W. I. and Znaniecki, F. (1927 edn) *The Polish peasant in Europe and America* (New York: Dover Publications)

Todorov, T. (1989) *Nous et les autres: la réflexion française sur la diversité humaine* (Paris: Editions du Seuil)

Topping, E. (1983) 'Patriarchal prejudice and pride in Greek Christianity – some notes on origins', *Journal of Modern Greek Studies*, Vol. 1, No. 1, pp.7-18

Tsaloumas, Dimitris (1983) *The observatory* (Brisbane: University of Queensland Press)

Tsoucalas, C. (1986) Lecture, Department of Modern Greek, University of Sydney, April 30

Turner, B. (1986) *The body and society* (Oxford: Basil Blackwell)

——(1987) 'Ageing, dying and death' in Turner, B. (ed.) *Medical power and social knowledge* (London: Sage)

Turpin, T. (1990) 'The social construction of immigrant and Aboriginal ethnic group boundaries in Australia', unpublished PhD thesis, La Trobe University, Melbourne

Van den Berghe, P. (1970) *Race and ethnicity: essays in comparative sociology* (New York: Basic Books)

Wallerstein, Immanuel (1974) *The modern world system* (New York: Academic Press)

Walwicz, Ania (1982) *Writing* (Melbourne: Rigmarole Books)

——(1983) 'Needle', *Meanjin*, Vol. 42, No. 1, March, p.27

Warner, L. (1936) 'American class and caste', *American Journal of Sociology*, Vol. XLII, Sept. 1936, pp.234–7

Warner, L. and Srole, L. (1945) *The social systems, of American ethnic groups* (New Haven: Yale University Press)

Williams, Raymond (1976) *Keywords* (London: Fontana)

——(1977) *Marxism and literature* (Oxford: Oxford University Press)

——(1978) *The second generation* (London: Chatto and Windus)

——(1981) *Culture* (Glasgow: Fontana)

Willis, P. (1981) *Learning to labour: how working class kids get working class jobs* (New York: Columbia University Press)

Willmott, P. (1966) *Adolescent boys of east London* (Baltimore: Penguin)

Wirth, L. (1928) *The ghetto* (Chicago: University of Chicago Press)

Wolf, Eric (1982) *Europe and the people without history* (Berkeley: University of California Press)

Yuval-Davis, N. and Anthias, F. (eds) (1989) *Women–nation–state* (London: Macmillan)

Zubrzycki, J. (1978) 'Immigration and the family in multicultural Australia', Meredith Memorial Lecture (Melbourne: La Trobe University)

——(1986) 'Multiculturalism and beyond: The Australian experience in retrospect and prospect' (paper presented to Australian Institute of Multicultural Affairs, 1986 National Research Conference, 14–16 May, University of Melbourne)

Index